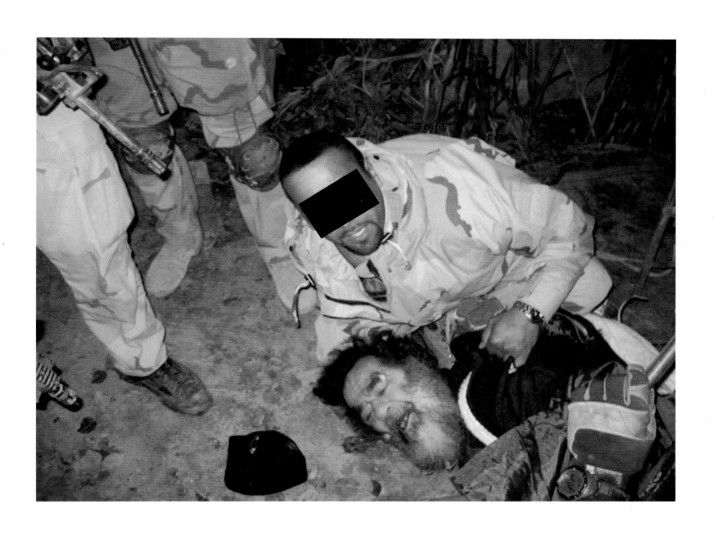

DELTA

AMERICA'S ELITE COUNTERTERRORIST FORCE

TERRY GRISWOLD and D. M. GIANGRECO

ZENITH PRESS

First published in 2005 by Zenith Press, an imprint of MBI Publishing Company, Galtier Plaza, Suite 200, 380 Jackson Street, St. Paul, MN 55101-3885 USA

Zenith Press titles are also available at discounts in bulk quantity for industrial or sales-promotional use. For details write to Special Sales Manager at MBI Publishing Company, Galtier Plaza, Suite 200, 380 Jackson Street, St. Paul, MN 55101-3885 USA.

ISBN 0-7603-2110-8

Editorial: Steve Gansen and Lindsay Hitch
Design: Brenda C. Canales

Printed in China

On the front cover: A special forces trooper demonstrates proper techniques for clearing rooms and buildings in a mock city at the Special Warfare Training Center, Fort Bragg, North Carolina. SF students learn how to approach, clear, and secure the cleared area as they proceed through a city-like environment.

On the frontispiece: Saddam Hussein is subdued after becoming "uncooperative" during his capture.

On the title page: A special forces trooper takes up the frog position during a practice jump.

On the back cover: (top) "Ma deuce"—the reliable .50-caliber machine gun—continues to provide outstanding service to the special operations community.

(bottom) A soldier provides outer security during a raid in Kirkuk.

About the authors:
Terry Griswold spent more than 20 years in U.S. Army Special Forces and military intelligence, and is currently a corporate consultant for special operations, counter-narcotics, and counterterrorism.

D. M. Giangreco has authored books and articles on subjects as wide-ranging as the Falkland Islands' sovereignty question and the decentralization of the former Soviet Air Force command and control structure.

Contents

This is another type of war, new in its intensity, ancient in its origins—war by guerrillas, subversive, insurgents, assassins . . . seeking victory by eroding and exhausting the enemy instead of engaging him.
—President John F. Kennedy, 1962

Since the first edition of DELTA —*America's Elite Counterterrorist Force* appeared, we have witnessed a steady rise in political and religious violence—narco-terrorism, wars and chaos in Afghanistan and Chechnya, and the tragedy of September 11, 2001. But the most significant change has been the potential ability of well-financed international terrorists to inflict immense human suffering and dislocations of society if they are not destroyed or kept on the defensive.

The ghastly events of September 11 shocked not only Americans but also the world. Shock, however, is not the same as disapproval. Many in the Middle East were overjoyed that such blows were struck against "The Great Satan," while others in Europe and elsewhere took a more subtle satisfaction in America's comeuppance.

How could this happen to the world's superpower? As President Kennedy stated in 1962, this is an ancient form of warfare—with very modern weapons—and has its roots in the period after World War II and the Korean War when a direct confrontation with the United States became less attractive to the Soviet Union and China. These countries increasingly turned to "wars of national liberation" as a means of expanding their influence while minimizing their own risk.

The success of Ho Chi Minh's revolution in 1954 and Fidel Castro's Cuban revolution in 1959 and the rising tide of insurgencies around the globe made it clear to the newly elected President Kennedy that the focus of communist expansionism continued to spread within the Third World. Kennedy firmly believed that the communist's ominous Cuban foothold in the Western Hemisphere could be countered by a program aimed at stimulating peaceful evolution instead of violent revolution. His response to the communists' challenge was the Alliance for Progress.

The Alliance for Progress was a serious effort to promote stability in Latin America through political reform and economic and social development, and it served as a model for similar U.S. commitments in other less-developed regions. Embryonic communist insurgencies threatened this evolutionary process, and Kennedy moved quickly to blunt their threats by devising and implementing a doctrine of counterrevolutionary warfare. More than 40 years later, the descendants of his elite, unconventional warriors continue to assist dozens of potential or fledgling democracies while specifically tasked, direct–action arms of the Army, Navy, and Air Force stand ready to fight an insidious byproduct of Third World instability and the end of the Cold War— international terrorism.

In the years following the Iran hostage crisis and the disaster at Desert I, a great deal has been written on the 1st Special Forces Operational Detachment– DELTA. Most of the focus has been on the origins of the failed rescue attempt, the major players, technical problems, and in some cases, the strategic and tactical leadership of the units involved. However, the guts and backbone of DELTA is the individual trooper.

Each individual who makes up DELTA displays personal initiative and works well as part of a team. They are mature, confident in themselves, their teammates, and their unit, and they are unquestioned experts in their craft. These qualities are the essence of DELTA.

This story examines counterterrorism (CT) training and operations from the viewpoint of the elite special operations team members who wade into the dirty business of counterterrorism to protect U.S. lives and interests.

In a free society, there is immense pressure on special operations units. Because of the clandestine nature of DELTA's mission, the full story of this extraordinary and sophisticated unit cannot be told, regardless of how important its unique capabilities and successes are to the ongoing war against international terrorism.

"Need to know" is the term most often used in the business of intelligence—especially clandestine and covert operations. In the decades before the September 11 attacks, this security requirement and DELTA's necessarily low visibility made it a potential target for budget cutters searching for a "quick fix." Such actions would have been disastrous. However, the events of September 11, 2001, firmly established America's counterterrorist forces as a requirement for the nation's survival.

Those connected with any aspect of the war on terrorism *must* use the same terms and have a fundamental understanding of their meanings if they are to operate effectively. Problems arise when certain words are mistakenly used interchangeably. An excellent example is the misuse of *antiterrorism* and *counterterrorism*. Antiterrorism (AT) operations are those actions and activities taken to keep a location or people from becoming a target for terrorist activities, such as airport screening and security guards stationed at critical areas. Whereas, counterterrorist (CT) operations—hostage rescue, thwarting attacks, attacking terrorist groups—take place after the terrorists have initiated activities and actions for an attack or carried out an attack.

The material presented here is based on the research and experiences of the authors and does not represent the positions or policies of any official, agency, or department of the United States government, or any other agency or government. Material contained herein was derived from unclassified publications and sources and is intended to neither confirm nor deny, officially or unofficially, the views of any government or agency.

Unaccredited photos were taken by U.S. armed forces personnel and are in the public domain. The names of DELTA troopers are classified and, unless otherwise noted, all names given for soldiers below the rank of colonel are pseudonyms.

Chapter 1

OUT OF THE DESERT

Sea Stallions receive preflight preparations on the deck of the USS *Nimitz*. The RH-53Ds had been freshly painted to mimic the look of Iranian helicopters and carried green, white, and red Iranian identification roundels to further confuse prying eyes.

Out of the Desert

The takeoff had to go right the first time. There would be no second chance. As the last item on the preflight list was checked off, the pilot revved up the EC-130E's Allison turboprops to gain maximum power. Releasing the already-straining brakes and pushing the throttles to the firewall, the pilot nursed his aircraft slowly forward out of the jumbled mass of wheel ruts furrowed deeply into the Iranian desert. The straining engines created a mini sandstorm that all but obliterated the ghastly funeral pyre they were leaving behind. Resembling some prehistoric bird of prey, the dark Hercules sluggishly lifted away from the makeshift desert runway and the disaster that Operation *Eagle Claw* had become.

This aircraft was one of the last special operations birds leaving Iran after the aborted rescue attempt to free American hostages in Teheran. Ayatollah Khomeini's Revolutionary Guards had held their 53 prisoners in the captured U.S. Embassy compound for nearly six months, and the half-dozen Hercules had been slated to play a key role in rescuing them. Now, as five heavily loaded aircraft flew into the early morning darkness, an EC-130E tanker and an RH-53D Sea Stallion helicopter lay blazing in the desert. Through the swirling sand, passengers could clearly see what they had never believed possible: failure. Despite well-laid plans, the team's efforts ended in an inferno of exploding ammunition and twisted, burning aircraft.

What happened at the refuel site code-named *Desert I* has been argued about and even embellished in a Hollywood adventure film, but the basic facts remain the same. The six special operations aircraft that penetrated Iran on the night of

RH-53D Sea Stallions from the USS *Nimitz* practice low-level formation flying before the attempted rescue of American hostages in Iran.

RH-53D Sea Stallions on the aft hangar bay of the USS *Nimitz* before launch.

A Sea Stallion's burned-out hulk at *Desert I. Wide World Photos*

Revolutionary Guard checkpoints in Teheran surreptitiously photographed by Army personnel. They are armed with a variety of 7.62mm Heckler & Koch G3 rifles manufactured in Iran under a license obtained from the West German firm. (A) A Revolutionary Guard is carrying several weapons to comrades up the street while (B) the mountains surrounding Teheran are clearly visible.

April 24–25, 1980, were configured either as tankers to refuel the Sea Stallion helicopters or as transports to bring in the assault teams and their ground support. After reaching the site, the mission was scrubbed, and the force had to prepare for exfiltration.

The decision to abort was made after three of the eight Sea Stallions either failed to reach *Desert I* or could not proceed due to mechanical difficulties. Not enough helicopters were available to carry out the mission, so there was nothing for the rotary and fixed-wing aircraft to do but return to their separate starting points. In preparation for the exfiltration, one of the RH-53Ds had to be repositioned. During that maneuver, the helicopter's main rotor smashed into the cockpit of a parked EC-130; both aircraft erupted into flame, and the explosions turned the stark desert night into a ghastly beacon. During the hasty evacuation of the site, the remaining Sea Stallions were left behind.

On board the EC-130E were members of America's newly formed counterterrorist unit, known simply as DELTA. The unit had been activated in November 1977 but was untested, or unblooded, as military professionals would say, and this was to be their first operational mission. But while the troopers anticipated that their baptism of fire would soon come in Teheran, they instead found themselves trapped in a terrifying inferno fed by thousands of gallons of aircraft fuel. As one of the survivors would later report, the DELTA Blue Team troopers and air crew from the stricken EC-130 struggled to "unass the muther" as best they could, bearing their injured with them.

Caught in the tanker's burning, smoke-filled cargo bay, Master Sergeant Leonard M. Harris was quickly overcome by smoke as he attempted to rescue an Air Force crewman. Luckily for both men, they were pulled from the burning plane by other members of DELTA.

Harris and the other survivors were loaded into various aircraft for the trip out. Now, as the last Hercules flew in a rough trail formation through the inky darkness toward the Indian Ocean and safety, Harris began to regain consciousness. Watery eyes fixed on a light on the cabin roof and then wandered down to scan the confusion around him in the crowded cargo bay. DELTA troopers, dressed in Levi's, boots, and black field jackets, were interspersed with air crews, combat control team members, and other support personnel. Some sat in stunned silence, still wearing their woolen naval watch caps, while others stripped off layers of body armor, web gear, and sweat-stained clothing. Checking his own physical condition, Harris was surprised that, despite his brush with death, the only damage that he was able

to perceive, other than a raw throat from smoke inhalation, was a singed field jacket and a relatively minor burn across the back of his left hand.

Looking down at his blackened field jacket, he absently picked at the melted tape that covered the only insignia on the assault teams' tactical uniforms: a small American flag sewn on the right sleeve. The troopers were to have displayed the flags after entering the embassy grounds so the hostages would readily follow them out during the exfiltration. After all, in their uniforms, the rescue team looked more like muggers in a New York subway than members of an elite counterterrorist unit.

Peering across the red-lighted cargo compartment, Harris realized that he and the rest of the passengers were just trying to get comfortable while riding on the bouncing fuel bladder covering the length of the plane. While team medical personnel provided aid, others appeared to be sorting out the recent events. Regaining a sense of stability, Harris was helped into a sitting position by another trooper. He noticed that his palms were wet with sweat, and not really knowing if it was from fear or just shock, he wiped them on his faded Levi's. Leaning his head back against the cold metal skin of the Hercules, he muttered, "Good ol' Herky Bird."

In the absence of fear and pain that fatigue brings, he began to reflect on the events that brought him to this situation. "How in the hell did I get in this mess?"

The Reception Committee

As the last of the special operations aircraft lifted off from the chaos of *Desert I*, another intense drama was taking place in the Iranian capital. From a clandestine communications site well outside Teheran, Dick Meadows, a highly decorated and skilled former Green Beret, received word of *Desert I*'s disaster. His vulnerable advance party of special forces soldiers had infiltrated the city only a few days earlier under various cover stories designed to hide all traces of their true identity and mission. But now events beyond their control had forced them to immediately execute their own escape and evasion plans.

Nearly six months before *Eagle Claw*, on November 4, 1979, subject-matter experts from all relevant military and civilian agencies were drawn together to form an ad hoc joint task force (JTF) charged with both the planning and execution of the hostage rescue. Unfortunately, though, interservice and interdepartmental bickering soon created coordination problems. The resulting problems—demonstrated by the initial lack of cooperation from the Central Intelligence Agency (CIA) and state department

A mass demonstration in Freedom Square on Eisenhower Avenue about a half-dozen miles west of the U.S. Embassy. In the unlikely event that Iranian mobs would react quickly enough to threaten the rescue mission, a circling AC-130H Specter gunship would perform crowd control around the embassy. It would also prevent armored vehicles—from an army ordnance depot to the north or the police headquarters near the Ministry of Foreign Affairs to the south—from intervening. If the Specter found itself hard pressed to keep the threats at bay, a second gunship covering Mehrabad International Airport to the west would destroy Iranian F-4 Phantom jets, capable of chasing down the rescue aircraft, and assist at the embassy.

officials—tended to frustrate rather than facilitate planning by the JTF's staff officers under the stewardship of Major General James B. Vought, a highly respected paratrooper with much experience working with Rangers.

Ideally, CIA operatives would have already been in the area of interest providing current intelligence and would have been obtaining critical items such as safe houses and locally procured trucks in Teheran. But the agency was undergoing a number of reorganizations prompted by highly publicized criticism of its role in major incidents going back as far as the Bay of Pigs invasion of Cuba. Sensational reports of alleged assassination attempts on foreign leaders, Vietnam's numerous "black" or covert operations (including the unjustly maligned *Phoenix* program), and the increasing number of former CIA employees who wrote tell-all books added to the growing public perception of a bumbling group of spies running amuck.

After Jimmy Carter assumed the presidency in 1977, he appointed a fellow Annapolis graduate, Admiral Stansfield Turner,

to oversee the restructuring of the CIA and the institution of his administration's "Georgia approach" to governmental management. Under Turner, hundreds of experienced personnel were laid off. The agency soon became heavily dependent on mechanical and technical means as the primary method of gathering intelligence instead of using those methods in conjunction with, or as a complement to, human intelligence (HUMINT) collection. By the time the embassy in Teheran was seized, Middle Eastern operations were in a major decline; in fact, the last full-time operative in Iran had already retired.

Despite the CIA's reinfiltration of one of its agents into Teheran, DELTA's thirst for intelligence on a broad range of matters was not satisfied. The black boxes were clearly failing to produce the information required to carry out this delicate operation, and the *Eagle Claw* planners in DELTA began to look within the special operations community for HUMINT collection means to make up the shortfall. The search led them to Dick Meadows.

A Revolutionary Guard bunker in central Teheran.

This was not the first time that Meadows had participated in an effort to free U.S. prisoners. Ten years before, he had been in charge of the compound assault team during Operation *Ivory Coast* (more commonly known as the Son Tay Raid), an airborne assault on a prisoner-of-war camp only 20 miles from Hanoi in North Vietnam.[*] Other exploits in Southeast Asia included the capture of North Vietnamese artillery pieces in Laos and the recapture of a major CIA outpost in that same country. Meadows was an expert in low-visibility insertions and takedowns.

Meadows had become a civilian advisor to DELTA after retiring from the Army, and his extensive background in clandestine cross-border operations, as well as his completion of the British Special Air Service (SAS) selection course, carried a great deal of weight in choosing him to enter Teheran ahead of the rescue force. Above all, the JTF planners knew Meadows could be trusted to do his best to accomplish the mission, and he knew DELTA inside and out. But all of that knowledge could be a problem if he were captured and interrogated.

Meadows' orders were to infiltrate Teheran, establish a safe house, procure local covered trucks for the rescue force, and guide the rescuers from the landing zone to their assault positions near the embassy. He was the reception committee and, on paper at

least, this was one of the less-complicated parts of the operation. One critical concern for Meadows was his cover—his background information and the story he fabricated to explain why he was in Teheran. CIA liaison officers supplied him with an Irish background, including all the necessary documentation and accessories, while the JTF provided additional backups and an enhanced language capability in the form of three sergeants recruited in Germany—two from Detachment A of the Berlin Brigade and one from the Air Force.

Unlike Meadows, these men already had covers and were conducting their daily lives under that blanket of anonymity. All were foreign-born nationals who had joined America's armed forces and were now U.S. citizens. One of the men was a native of Germany and was intimately acquainted with the murky world of working with and supporting intelligence requirements levied on the Army by other agencies such as the CIA. Another of the operatives was born in Great Britain and was easily cloaked with the mantle of a Scottish background. The third (who had undergone no previous special forces training) was a native of the Middle East and was fluent in Farsi, the primary language of Iran. These men would provide Meadows with the additional skills the advance party required.

[*]Over four dozen U.S. prisoners were held at the camp but were moved shortly before the raid and remained in captivity until after the 1973 signing of the Paris Peace Accords. One side benefit of the operation, however, was an accidental attack on a nearby compound that apparently killed as many as 200 Chinese, East Block, or Soviet specialists involved in upgrading North Vietnam's air defenses.

When it was discovered late in the planning that three high-ranking hostages were being held in the Ministry of Foreign Affairs building six miles from the embassy, an additional 13 soldiers were assigned from Detachment A in Berlin. There wasn't enough time to change the basic plan and shift existing personnel to other targets, so these men had to fill the operational void created by the last-minute intelligence. Special forces detachments like theirs had been preparing to fight potential Soviet invaders in the extensively built-up areas of western Germany since the late 1950s and were composed of experts in urban warfare.

Eagle Claw's mission profile called for the advance team to rendezvous with the DELTA rescue force staging out of a little-used airfield near Qena, 300 miles south of Cairo in central Egypt. Upon receipt of the execution message, the 132 men of the rescue force and additional support personnel flew on two C-141s from Egypt to an air base operated by British and Omani personnel on the large Arabian Sea island of Misirah. At the same time, the helicopter element on the aircraft carrier USS *Nimitz* "patrolling" nearby in the Gulf of Oman prepared to launch its RH-53D helicopters to an isolated spot, code-named *Desert I*, in Iran's Dasht-e Karir (Salt

A force of a dozen U.S. Army Rangers and DELTA members made up two teams to secure the road running through the *Desert I* refuel site. Ranger and DELTA troopers armed with a Colt M16 assault rifle and Walther MP-L submachine gun peered intently throughout the night. The relatively heavy PVS-5 night-vision goggles could only be worn for about 30 minutes before a pilot or trooper would have to hand it off to a designated partner to wear. Within minutes after they rode their Yamaha motorcycles out of the belly of the first MC-130 to land, the team captured a bus with 44 Iranian civilians, blew up a gasoline tanker truck with a light antitank weapon, and ran off another truck. Although *Eagle Claw* planners were later criticized for establishing the refuel site in a moderately traveled area, mission parameters left them little choice, and DELTA planned to fly any Iranians taken into custody back to Misirah Island on the returning MC-130s. The Iranians would then be flown back to Iranian territory and released at Manzariyeh Air Base the following night. If the mission had been aborted after they had been flown from *Desert I*, the Iranians would have been turned over to the International Red Cross for repatriation.

Desert). Also, a contingent of four AC-130E and H Specter gunships was readied for launch the following night; they would fly directly from Qena to Teheran to support the rescue. The Specters would be refueled by KC-135 tankers as they passed over Saudi Arabia.

The next phase of the operation called for DELTA's surgical assault force, along with its security and support element, to take off from Misirah in EC-130Es and MC-130Es of the 8th Special Operations Squadron. Their destination, *Desert I*, had already been surveyed by an Air Force combat control team member who placed remotely operated infrared beacons along the hasty landing strip. After the force successfully rendezvoused at *Desert I* near Garmsar, 265 nautical miles southeast of Teheran, the assault element was to load onto the helicopters and fly on to *Desert II* in

the rugged, mountainous region just southeast of the capital. Once there, the choppers would be hidden nearby, at a site code-named *Figbar*, while the assault force linked up with the reception committee before dawn.

The assault force would settle in for the day while the DELTA commander, Colonel Charlie A. Beckwith, would infiltrate Teheran with 12 select troopers who would receive the trucks gathered by Meadows' team near the city at a secure warehouse called the Mushroom. It was their job to drive the small convoy out of the city on the second night of the operation and collect the rest of the rescue force from the hide site. After transferring to the six large tarpaulin-covered Mercedes trucks and a Volkswagen van, 106 DELTA and special forces troopers would journey to the capital where final preparations for the impending rescue would be made.

An M151 roars over a sand dune in Egypt. The soldiers given the mission of guarding the dirt road running through *Desert I* were not picked until after the main body of Rangers, slated to seize Manzariyeh Air Base, had arrived at Qena, Egypt. Intensive training immediately began for both the road-watch and airfield-seizure teams.

The plan called for the rescue force to depart from *Desert II* at 2030 hours and be in their designated assault positions by 2300 hours. Meadows would take Colonel Beckwith on a personal reconnaissance of the target before the attack at approximately the same time that the AC-130s were lifting off in Egypt.

The main assault group's three teams (code-named *Red*, *White*, and *Blue*) and Foreign Ministry assault group would use the principles of surprise, shock, and coordinated movement to take out Ayatollah's Revolutionary Guards. As soon as the short, violent rescue operation erupted at the walled embassy compound, the hidden RH-53D helicopters would emerge from their camouflaged position near *Desert II*. One would head for the large park surrounding the Foreign Ministry, while the rest would fly to sites at the rear of the embassy compound and the Amjedeih soccer stadium across the street, where both hostages and rescuers would be picked up. If the compound site couldn't be cleared of obstructions in time, all extractions would be conducted from the stadium.

Throughout the ground phase of the operation, one AC-130 gunship would orbit over the target area providing fire support, and another would cover the two Iranian F-4 Phantom jets on strip alert at Teheran's nearby Mehrabad International Airport. Two additional Specters would orbit close by in reserve. All parties concerned were fully confident that the massive firepower the Specters could bring to bear on the surrounding area would be more than enough to suppress any Revolutionary Guards attempting to reinforce their embassy security force and prevent the infamous Iranian mobs from interfering with the rescue. As one of the gunship pilots would later explain, the Specters' awesome firepower was the "best crowd-control measure" available.

While the AC-130s dominated the area, the helicopters would leave the chaos of Teheran for nearby Manzariyeh Air Base only 35 minutes away. Manzariyeh was to have already been secured by a 75-man ranger contingent and support personnel flying directly from Qena in four MC-130s. This elite light infantry unit was composed of experts in airfield seizure. Using M151s and commercial off-road motorcycles, they were capable of gobbling up the sprawling but lightly defended facility in a matter of minutes.

Throughout the exfiltration, F-14A Tomcat fighters and KA-6D Intruder tankers from the USS *Nimitz* would orbit over

Before operations could begin, Air Force ground personnel had to be flown into both Qena and the British Omani air base on Misirah Island to set up communications and logistics for the 34 special operations tankers, transports, and gunships involved in *Eagle Claw*.

Persian Gulf waters—on call to knock down any hostile aircraft coming after the vulnerable transports and gunships leaving Manzariyeh. If all went well, the entire force—Rangers, special forces, Meadows' team, support personnel, DELTA, and their newly rescued charges—would be quickly loaded aboard a pair of C-141s, which had made a quick dash from Dhahran, Saudi Arabia, and exfiltrated to Qena before the Iranians could take any effective countermeasures. There was no way to fly the helicopters out of Iran, and they were to be destroyed before the last Rangers left the airfield.

The catastrophe at *Desert I* changed all that. After Meadows received word over a clandestine radio to abort the mission, he notified the team, which dispersed from the safe house, and all made their individual ways to the passenger terminal at Teheran's Mehrabad International Airport. Security within the terminal was visibly increased. Unshaven and clad in an irregular mix of civilian and military clothing, the pride of Iran's Revolutionary Guard nervously paced back and forth near entrances, fingering their newly acquired Heckler & Koch G3 rifles. The menacing looks—as well as a healthy respect for the weapons' stopping power—caused

Meadows to give each of the guards a grudging deference. Swallowing hard, Meadows entered the terminal entrance and walked directly to the Swiss Air ticket counter. Very deliberately, and somewhat slowly, he reached into the inner pocket of his corduroy jacket for the cash necessary to open the first of many doors to the waiting jet and freedom.

While being processed, he noticed that his Scottish comrade was in another part of the terminal, being questioned by Revolutionary Guards, customs officials, and soldiers. Meadows later learned that the large amount of U.S. currency that brought this unwanted attention to the Scotsman stayed in Iran with that group of officials. The newfound hatred of the Great Satan obviously did not extend to financial matters, and well-placed bribes of American greenbacks continued to do the trick.

Reaching down to retrieve his carryall, Meadows realized that despite the fact that word had been received about an "invasion" to the south, security efforts at the airport remained disjointed and uncoordinated. Walking at a casual but determined pace toward the Swiss Air jet, he wondered what things were like at the embassy.

Chapter 2

A NEW GAME IN TOWN

Kill one and terrorize a thousand.
—Sun Tzu, 500 B.C.

One of the terrorists holding Israeli athletes at the Munich Olympics relays demands to German negotiators in front of millions of television viewers.

estering Arab resentment of America's direct and substantial support of Israel grew steadily after the United States became the Jewish state's chief sponsor in the wake of the 1967 Six Day War. By 1973, when massive American arms shipments played a critical role in blocking an Egyptian-Syrian victory in the Yom Kippur War, the United States was firmly planted on a collision course with the rising tide of pan-Arab nationalism. From this point forth, Americans would no longer be incidental victims of terrorist attacks. They would be the targets.

During the Six Day War, the sweeping successes of the Israeli military made it clear to the Arab world that change could not be guaranteed by conventional forces alone. And watching from the sidelines with great interest were millions of Palestinians living in forced exile in the Middle East and in Europe. At the same time, the United States was preoccupied with the Vietnam War, the civil rights movement, and growing campus unrest. Against this backdrop, the United States hoped that every effort would be made to solve the numerous long-standing issues in the Middle East peacefully. Failing

Television crews and reporters line the balcony of the Beirut International Airport during the nine-day hijacking of a TWA jet, June 22, 1985. The media was—and continues to be—one of international terrorism's most important weapons. *Wide World Photos*

The grand finale of the Palestine Liberation Operation's September 1970 hijacking of three civilian airliners. Their 300 passengers were held for a week and, after their release, the aircraft were blown up at an abandoned airfield near Amman, Jordan.

that, the U.S. hoped that disagreements could be prevented from boiling over into open warfare. But the Palestinian issue exploded to the surface, amid smoke and gunfire, in the Hashemite kingdom of Jordan.

Cornered by Soviet-sponsored, Syrian-armed Palestinian forces intent on using his country as a staging area for raids on Israel, King Hussein ibn-Talal used his army to drive the Palestinians into Syria and reasserted his authority. The king and his Hashemite followers had never enjoyed an easy relationship with the various *fedayeen* groups making up Yasser Arafat's Palestine Liberation Organization (PLO), and its military arm, the Fatah, which was openly encroaching on the country's control of the Jordan River Valley. One faction, George Habbash's Popular Front for the Liberation of Palestine (PFLP)—the largest and most anti-Hashemite of the fedayeen—had worked

feverishly to undermine Hussein's throne long before the bloody confrontation.

The intense fighting for the capital of Amman and across northern Jordan in September 1970 caused great concern in the West, and a number of countries sent supplies. Military forces were also alerted to move in and provide help, but the Jordanian army succeeded without them. This stunning defeat of the Fatah-led Palestinians, however, laid the groundwork for the emergence of full-fledged terrorist organizations such as Black September, a radical group that operated as an arm of the "moderate" PLO until it split off on its own. The name itself commemorates the fedayeen's expulsion from Jordan, and they took their revenge on the man who directed King Hussein's forces, Premier Wafsi Tal, by assassinating him the following year in Cairo.

While terrorists have never hesitated to murder any Arab leader who wasn't in strict agreement with their particular

As an instructor looks on, a member of SAS takes position and returns fire against mock terrorists during a training exercise. He is positioned behind the engine block, which can provide adequate protection against most conventional pistol and rifle ammunition.

dogma, it usually isn't considered acceptable to blame other Arabs for their numerous defeats by Israel. The fledgling terrorists saw the Western world as the cause of virtually all Arab problems—perceived or real—and several factors combined to make Western Europe an excellent target for their activities: Western Europe was close to the Middle East, and its open societies gave the terrorists a remarkable degree of freedom to carry out their activities.

Terrorists' threats to use violence against individuals to affect a much larger, related group is not a new phenomenon; what is called terrorism today is a tactic of warfare that's been employed throughout history.

These new terrorists were also media-savvy and fully understood the ramifications of the revolution in global telecommunications. Advances in television technology allowed them to move beyond the printed word and see their heinous acts broadcast to much of the world's population. Ratings-conscious news agencies and the viewers themselves had enabled the television camera to become one of the terrorists' chief weapons.

Bombing, hijacking, assassination, and kidnapping are types of terrorist warfare magnified a thousand-fold by the electronic media. In the early 1970s, the world was introduced to new television stars such as Black September[*] and the

[*]One of the many organization names used by Sabri Khalil al-Banna (alias Abu Nidal) in an effort to create confusion in the West and make the armed struggle against Israel appear larger than it was. In addition to Black September, other names used by the Abu Nidal organization include: Fatah Revolutionary Council, Black June Organization, the Arab Revolutionary Brigades, and the Revolutionary Organization of Socialist Muslims.

Baader-Meinhoff Gang. In 1970, several commercial airliners were hijacked and taken with their 300 passengers and crew to Dawson Field, a desert airfield 40 miles from Amman formerly used by Britain's Royal Air Force. After a week, the hostages were removed from the aircraft, which were then blown up in full view of the world. But the event that had the deepest and most far-reaching impact was the drama that unfolded at the 1972 Olympic Games in Munich, West Germany.

Television viewers were stunned by images of the wanton murder of innocents, and governments in the West soon felt the power to control events slipping from their hands. Terrorist actions—or even the threat of such actions—were increasingly shaping policy decisions.

Some ramifications of these terrorist attacks not observed by the public were the new requirements placed on international law enforcement and military forces. After failing to negotiate for the release or rescue of the Israeli athletes, West Germany's security needs were scrutinized from every possible angle with Teutonic efficiency. And the realists who would have to face the next round of fighting concluded that virtually every Western nation was now in the battle with this ancient form of warfare. The emergence of a new combatant—the counterterrorist—was Western Europe's response.

Each country dealt with terrorism based on how its own political, economic, social, and religious situation affected its security. Germany established a special unit within its border police—GSG-9, short for Grenzschutzgruppe 9—and the French formed the Groupe d'Intervention de la Gendarmerie National (GIGN). The British turned to their old standby, the SAS, while the U.S. decided to wait and see, with the attitude that, "This will not happen to us." Yet, through the early 1970s, it was painfully obvious that terrorists were moving a step or two ahead of the various national security forces and could attack whenever or wherever they wanted. The counterterrorist groups would soon prove, however, that they too were forces to be reckoned with.

In October 1977, at Mogadishu Airport in Somalia, Germany's GSG-9 exacted revenge for the tragedy at Munich by foiling a terrorist hijacking. Unknown to the terrorists, the Germans had learned much from the tragedy of Munich, and with the help of two SAS commandos who blew open the aircraft's doors, a 30-man GSG-9 force stormed the plane during the early morning hours. Later, in May 1980, the SAS gained international fame by conducting one of the most daring and highly publicized hostage rescues to date—Pagoda Troop of B Squadron, 22nd SAS Regiment, launched a spectacular assault on the Iranian Embassy in London as television cameras broadcast the action around the world.

Preceding these events was the most famous rescue operation of the period: the raid on Entebbe Airport in Uganda, conducted by the Israeli special forces. Launched from bases within their own borders more than 2,500 miles to the north, the commandos of Unit 269 flew directly into the site where 103 hostages were held. In the early morning darkness of July 4, 1976, Operation *Thunderbolt* was carried out with clockwork precision. Keeping it simple, the rescue force landed in four C-130s. The lead Hercules casually taxied to within 200 yards of the terminal building holding the hostages, and a black Mercedes sedan rolled down the ramp. The sedan cruised up to the brightly lit building, followed by a pair of nondescript Land Rovers, and suddenly disgorged nine Unit 269 commandos.

Within minutes, the Israeli strike force had secured the terminal area and airfield perimeter, removing a potential problem by blowing up the Ugandan MiG fighter aircraft, and then loaded up the rescued hostages. The rescue force commander, Colonel Jonathan Netanyahu*, was killed, as well as the entire terrorist gang and an undetermined number of Ugandan soldiers protecting the captors. All but one of the hostages, an elderly woman who had been taken to a hospital and later murdered, were quickly freed and flown to Nairobi, Kenya, where the injured were transferred to a waiting jet airliner equipped for medical emergencies.

Americans Become Targets

The United States entered the counterterrorism (CT) arena as a very unwilling participant, primarily due to its deeply engrained separation of military and police powers and the

* The colonel's brother, Captain Benjamin Netanyahu, later became a leading figure in Israeli politics, including prime minister (1996–1999) and minister of foreign affairs (2002–present).

The aftermath of a Red Army Faction car bomb explosion at Rhein-Main Air Base outside Frankfurt, West Germany, August 8, 1985. Over 20 people were injured, and the blast killed one U.S. airman and the wife of another. The explosives were packed into a car with forged U.S. license plates and driven to the parking lot outside the headquarters of the 435th Tactical Air Wing. It is believed that the terrorist who drove the vehicle gained access to the base by using the identification card of a U.S. serviceman murdered the previous night.

resultant conservative approach of U.S. military leaders to what they felt was a police problem. Neither the political nor military hierarchies originally supported the view held by many in the lower echelons that media-savvy terrorists were an increasing threat to the United States and its interests.

U.S. intelligence agencies learned their first direct lessons from the new terrorists in the September 1970 uprising in Jordan. It was feared that Fatah insurgents would seize the U.S. Embassy in Amman, and U.S. paratroopers were alerted to, if necessary, seize the airport, land an armed force, and retake the embassy.

As with Operation *Eagle Claw* some 10 years later, the Jordanian rescue plan was complicated, unwieldy, and fraught with unnecessary risks. For example, the 509th Airborne Infantry, which was selected to seize the airport, would have had to fly to Jordan via an extremely lengthy, circuitous route from their staging area in West Germany. Instead of taking the normal route over continental Europe to reach the eastern Mediterranean, their operational plan called for a flight over

Pistols

Stopping power, mass versus velocity, number of rounds versus weight—the argument seems never-ending, but over time, weapons firing the 9mm (.38-caliber) round have become respected additions to DELTA's arsenal.

Modern conventional warfare generally calls for lightweight, high-velocity rounds such as the Colt M16's .223-caliber/5.56mm or NATO's standard .308-caliber/7.62mm that are effective to several hundred yards. For the takedown of a hostage-holding site, however, 100 feet is considered an extreme range. Counterterrorists need a heavy slug that will knock a man down with as few shots as possible, and rounds smaller than .45-caliber have often proven to be inadequate against a determined enemy. As early as the beginning of the twentieth century, Moro warriors battling U.S. soldiers in the Philippines were not stopped by government-issue .38-caliber pistols and, most recently, in the GSG-9 operation against aircraft hijackers at Mogadishu, Somalia, the German commander was forced to empty his snub-nosed .38-caliber into a psyched-up terrorist who continued to fight even as six bullets ripped into his body. For this reason, many operatives prefer to have a bigger weapon.

A big (very big) round like that from the Smith & Wesson .44-caliber Magnum will drop a hijacker in his tracks but will also likely penetrate its intended target as well as several seats and passengers before it stops. Moreover, the .44 Magnum's substantial recoil can delay firing the next shot—possibly with disastrous results. The .45-caliber ACP round fired by the Colt or Springfield Armory M1911A1 automatic pistols has a great advantage over its famous friend during takedowns. Its low muzzle velocity, at roughly 830 feet per second, is about half that of the .44 Magnum, and hostage safety is greatly increased since there is more likelihood that the captors' bodies will stop the bullets.

But while this would seem to make the .45 the weapon of choice for takedowns, many shooters have gravitated to the 9mm Beretta Model 92 pistol. The high velocity of its 9mm parabellum slug is easily brought below 1,000 feet per second by reducing the round's charge, and, depending on which variant of the Model 92 is used, the counterterrorist can make almost twice as many shots before reloading than if he carried a conventional .45-caliber automatic.

The Colt automatic pistol and the higher-quality product manufactured by Springfield Armory, normally fires from eight- and seven-bullet magazines, respectively, and each can carry an additional round in the chamber, while the Model 92 and its variants have 13- and 15-round magazines. The tradeoff is that while 9mm bullets are indeed smaller, their size is adequate and the Model 92 has more of them. Moreover, the ammunition a DELTA trooper carries on his body and in his weapon is all that he can count on during a takedown. If everything goes as planned, there will be very little shooting. But if the operation goes sour, it's just DELTA and the terrorists in a high-intensity shootout of unknown duration. Frequently, the first side to run out of bullets loses and, with a weight nearly half that of a .45-caliber bullet, a lot of 9mm rounds can be carried without encumbering a trooper.

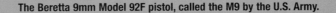

The Beretta 9mm Model 92F pistol, called the M9 by the U.S. Army.

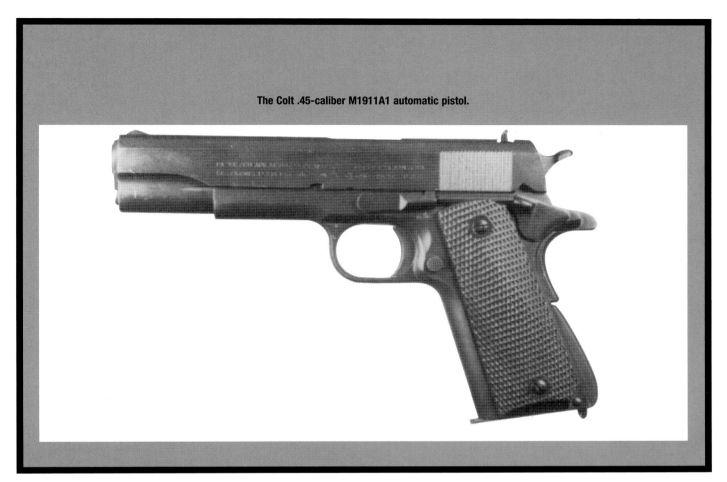

The Colt .45-caliber M1911A1 automatic pistol.

the North Sea and the Atlantic Ocean around Spain to the Gibraltar slot, and then across the length of the Mediterranean. The force would have to take this roundabout route because NATO allies wouldn't grant overflight rights—a situation unpleasantly similar to what F-111 pilots would find 16 years later during a retaliatory raid on Libya for sponsoring a terrorist bombing.

U.S. planners were faced with a number of similar situations over the next two years, and missions were not approved. Either White House or state department jitters prevented airborne and special forces units from launching counterterrorist assaults. Terrorist networks in the Middle East, however, could easily strike soft targets and continued to target Israeli citizens. Americans stationed in Germany, as well as West Germans, found themselves the targets of former antiwar students turned terrorists. In May 1972 the Baader-Meinhoff Gang, also known as the Red Army Faction, finally forced the issue on the United States by conducting six separate bombings. Their targets were the U.S. officers' club in Frankfurt and the U.S. Army Europe Headquarters in Heidelberg. The media provided some coverage of these

strikes, but it was minimal compared to the extensive coverage of the Munich Olympic Games.

While facing the capture of American hostages wasn't yet a problem, perceptive military leaders realized that the United States needed to be ready and able to respond to terrorism, and units within the Army's special forces community were tasked with conducting rescues using the hasty option response. In lay terms, this means that if captors begin to harm their hostages, the team attempts a quick, efficient rescue. But the hasty response doesn't allow for the meticulous planning, coordination, and rehearsal typically needed by CT units to execute surgical strikes, so CT units hope they'll never have to conduct them.

Soon after Munich, American military and civilian advisors recommended that a suitable force be established to fight terrorism. But it wasn't until the increased threat was demonstrated to President Jimmy Carter and the feasibility of creating a unit like those that struck at Entebbe and Mogadishu that the United States acknowledged the need to establish its own full-time, state-of-the-art counterterrorist response unit. Operation *Thunderbolt*'s success further confirmed what many planners

Automatic Weapons

Although pistols are preferred in most hostage situations, submachine guns are needed when large target areas or many terrorists (four or more) are involved. Delta initially settled on the domestically produced .45-caliber M3A1 "grease gun," a World War II-vintage weapon that went out of production in the early 1950s and was generally shunned by the Army. But the same features that made it unpopular also made it an effective tool for room-clearing: a low muzzle velocity that allowed its heavy slugs to slam into—not through—a terrorist, and a rate of fire slow enough to shoot off single shots without disturbing the shooter's aim. The M3A1 is now obsolete due to a lack of replacement parts, but has made way for a variety of submachine guns.

Selection of weapons is a personal choice that often involves weight, accuracy, cleaning frequency, ammo per magazine, and reliability after it has survived a parachute jump. The Heckler & Koch MP5 and the less-expensive easily concealed Walther MP-K are both German arms that fire 9mm rounds, as does the Colt submachine gun that shares many parts with the M16 rifle. The compact Colt Model 733 Commando assault rifle, now standardized as the M4, also benefits from this commonality and can be used on missions requiring its higher velocity 5.56mm round.

An M4 fitted with sound suppressor, Aimpoint sight, and high-intensity light awaits it operator in Kosovo.

Colt 9mm submachine gun.

The General Motors Guide Lamp Division .45-caliber M3 submachine gun often described as "a pleasant gun to shoot."

An old stand-by from the Vietnam era: the Colt 5.56mm Model 733 Commando assault rifle. Its sister, the Model 727, is today standardized with minor modifications as the popular M4 carbine assault rifle.

The Walther 9mm MP-K submachine gun, which served as a useful bridge between the M3 and the MP5.

The basic Colt 5.56mm M16A4 assault rifle.

The Heckler & Koch 9mm MP5 submachine gun.

The Heckler & Koch MP5 SD3 fires 9mm ammo and, with its collapsing stock and integral silencer, is an outstanding weapon for the close-in fight. The sound suppressor is a two-stage external silencer. The first stage of the system absorbs gases while the second absorbs the muzzle blast and flame. The bolt noise is absorbed by buffers made of rubber. If you use subsonic ammo, the report can be heard more than 15 to 20 feet away.

Grenades

The familiar "pineapple," properly known as the Mk II fragmentation hand grenade, was pulled from Army frontline service over a decade before DELTA was formed. A cylindrical canister about the size of a shaving cream can is used for concussion grenades, chemical grenades (such as tear gas), and flash/bang grenades. This design allows the grenade's user to gently roll it a predictable direction and distance into a room, unlike the Mk II and similar grenades, which could wobble almost anywhere—including back up against the very wall that a trooper is using for shelter! Before the relatively recent fielding of the flat-sided M560 series fragmentation grenades, if a mission profile called for use of an antipersonnel grenade with a predictable roll, an M57 or M61 would have to be soldered into an appropriately sized tin can to achieve the desired effect. Once the pin was pulled and the safety lever fell away, a nearly perfect roll could be achieved every time.

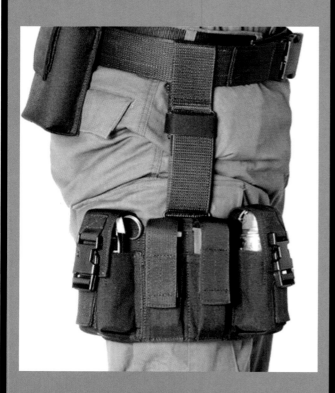

Flash-bang grenades with no-snag caps in an Eagle Industries hip pouch. Center pockets hold clips for 9mm Heckler & Koch submachine guns.

Armed with a Colt Model 727 carbine, a DELTA trooper pulls personal protection duty during Operation *Desert Storm*. Note the trooper's sterile uniform (no identification or other markings) and long hair. A three-power telescopic site is mounted on the carbine.

already knew: the United States needed a small surgical force capable of carrying out such operations. It was their contention that, despite the claims of the airborne community, ranger companies and battalions were neither trained nor equipped for hostage rescues.

From the smoke of military infighting and political intrigue, 1st Special Forces Operational Detachment–DELTA was formed in 1977. Six ALPHA detachments (A teams),

British Special Air Service

Great Britain's 22nd Special Air Service (SAS) and U.S. Special Forces have enjoyed a long, close relationship that began in earnest during the late 1950s. Lieutenant General Sir Charles Richardson, Britain's director general of military training, inspects an SAS unit during an exercise with the 5th and 7th Special Forces Groups at Camp Troy, North Carolina, September 28, 1962. General Richardson's visit turned out to be a pivotal event for the SAS. While the conservative British military establishment had grudgingly conceded the regiment's value in certain situations, the unit was generally thought of as little more than a private army of ill-disciplined mavericks that skimmed some of Britain's best soldiers from the top of traditional regiments. A tour with the SAS could kill a young officer's career.

At Camp Troy and Fort Bragg, Richardson witnessed SAS troopers studying advanced demolition and field medicine techniques and engaging in specialized training in foreign languages and a worldwide assortment of weapons. He left North Carolina greatly impressed with what he saw, and the almost immediate improvement in the attitude of the British military establishment toward the SAS was credited to the general's glowing report.

The same month that General Richardson visited SAS elements training in the United States, the U.S. Special Forces soldier who would later found DELTA, Charlie Beckwith, led a troop from A Squadron, SAS, in a combined exercise with the French "paras" of the 1st Batallion de Parachutistes de Choc in Corsica. Beckwith had been attached to the regiment as part of an ongoing exchange program and would ship out to Malaya with the SAS to take part in deep jungle penetration missions against guerrillas along the Thai border in 1963. The tour nearly cost him his life, but upon his return to Fort Bragg, he pushed hard to have SAS training and organizational techniques adopted by special forces.

Shotguns

Shotguns are useful in a variety of situations but are most commonly associated with forced-entry techniques. Heavy rifled slugs can supply the pure smashing power needed to quickly and efficiently blow the hinges off most doors. Sabot rounds allow deeper target penetration and are best employed against vehicle or aircraft engines and door-locking mechanisms. After entry has been gained, shotguns can also be used against the hostage takers.

The Mossberg 12-gauge Cruiser 500 shotgun.

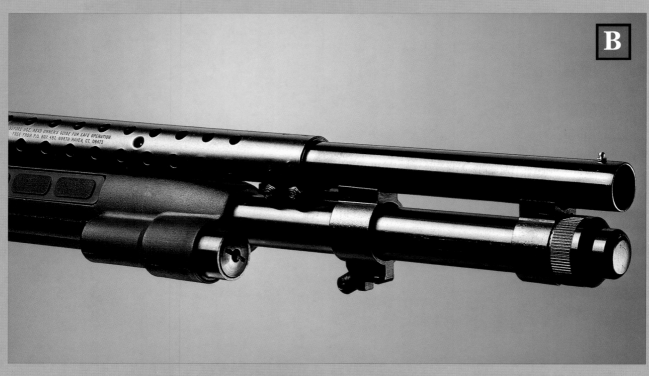

A Task Force Falcon soldier searching for Saddam Hussein wields a 12-gauge shotgun equipped with an external high beam light mounted under the barrel.

When DELTA was formed, its armorers developed special lighting equipment that could be attached to weapons for night operations. Today, such devices can be obtained off-the-shelf from manufacturers or are integral to the weapons. (A) A Hensoldt aiming point projector fitted to a Heckler & Koch MP5 A2 submachine gun and (B) a laser pointer built into the firearm of a Mossberg 12-gauge shotgun. Also note the Stabo rings attached to the soldier's tactical vest and the flash-bang grenade (an SAS invention) ready for use in his left hand.

Ammunition

When choosing ammunition, CT specialists want a man-stopper that will knock a terrorist down and keep him down. While the heavy .45-caliber slug remains ideal for hostage situations, the lethality of smaller slugs, like the 9mm, can be greatly enhanced by using soft-point bullets with hollow or flat tips, which expand the soft lead slug into a broad mushroom-shaped projectile upon entering the body, increasing its shock effect dramatically.

The rules of engagement in most wars prohibit the use of such ammunition, but DELTA troopers participating in a hostage rescue are not subject to the restrictions of the Geneva Convention. Like their police counterparts, they can legally use hollow-point ammunition (or exploding rounds that shatter on impact) to subdue captors and save the lives of hostages.

Advances in technology have complicated matters for DELTA and other CT specialists by adding dangerous new weapons such as handguns and bombs with almost no metal parts. Initially, only law enforcement agencies and the military had access to lightweight Kevlar body armor (which, incidentally, does not set off metal detectors). But now this highly effective armor is readily available to terrorist organizations. When worn in thin, easily concealable layers, Kevlar will stop the low-velocity slugs normally required for passenger safety. Technology and tactics have provided solutions to these and other problems but the decades-old argument over the most appropriate weapons to use will die harder than any flesh-and-blood fanatic.

Flat-point (A) and conventional (B) bullets.

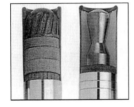

A 12-gauge rifled slug (left) and 12-gauge sabot slug (right).

commanded by captains, make up a company-sized BRAVO detachment (B team), commanded by a major. A CHARLIE detachment (C team) is a battalion-sized organization commanded by a lieutenant colonel. Since the 1st Special Forces Operational Detachment was commanded by a full colonel and structured along completely separate lines, following the squadron-troop structure of Britain's famed SAS, it became a DELTA detachment. Using the concept of the troop and the squadron as the building block or base, it initially trained to conduct counterterrorist operations. Activities in Iraq and Kuwait, however, revealed that DELTA's one-dimensional media image of a super-secret counterterrorist team fell well short of reality.

Charlie A. Beckwith of DELTA, circa 1979.

DELTA and *Blue Light*

Both DELTA's sponsors and opponents within the military held firm to ideas on who should respond to the terrorist challenge. Most of DELTA's sponsors were typical of America's military leadership. They were conservative officers who were slow to respond to the terrorist threat, but once convinced that the threat was real, they were bulldogs in their support of the unit. And those who had worked hard to undermine or sidetrack

DELTA (primarily because they didn't acknowledge the reality of the threat) eventually offered their full support.

Army Chief of Staff General Bernard Rogers, an astute Kansan and Rhodes scholar, watched as the armies of Great Britain and West Germany rapidly adopted what most American policymakers thought of as police powers normally kept out of the military's hands. After the Carter White House made it clear that it wanted a unit with specialized capabilities, Rogers approved DELTA's formation and told senior planners that he wanted the unit operational—now!

The person most instrumental in DELTA's early development was Lieutenant General Edward C. "Shy" Meyer. As the deputy chief of staff for operations, he was one of the most influential senior officers in the Army, and his office issued the plans and policies for how the U.S. Army would operate. General Meyer took a direct, personal interest in DELTA. From the first discussions about the need for a U.S. counterterrorist force through its birth and Operation *Eagle Claw*, Meyer always provided guidance and support. The rest of the Army may have called him Shy, but to DELTA he was Moses, parting the waters for his people.

General William DePuy, commander of the Training and Doctrine Command, was another DELTA supporter. General DePuy was *the* expert in training. Even though he was a conventional soldier, he recognized that a force "like the SAS" was needed (as he often said in major policy meetings). He had to be won over before General Rogers and others, but that proved easy after inquiries about similar organizations in Europe demonstrated that an effective CT unit could be formed within the U.S. Army. General DePuy would provide the training support.

DELTA's architect was the commandant of the special forces school: a gruff veteran of the guerrilla wars in Southeast Asia named Colonel Charlie Beckwith. Not only did Chargin' Charlie have a wealth of experience in unconventional operations, but he also knew who the power brokers were and how to use them. In 1975, when General "Iron Mike" Healy was reassigned from his command at the John F. Kennedy Special Warfare Center at Fort Bragg, his replacement was Major General Robert "Barbed Wire Bob" Kingston. Kingston's association with Beckwith went back to the days when Beckwith was an exchange officer with the SAS and Kingston was with the British Parachute Regiment. The two had also just served together at the Joint Casualty Resolution Center in Nakhon Phanom, Thailand, in 1973–1974. Kingston would work closely with General Meyer to establish an SAS-type unit.

During Colonel Beckwith's tour as commandant, the special operations community watched Europe's response to the outrages of various extremist groups. In an area known as Smoke Bomb Hill, special forces members refined their traditional skills and added the hasty-response operations to their repertoire. Special forces, however, had to carry out a wide range of missions and could not dedicate much of their training to hostage rescues.

Other soldiers lent their guidance and support during this critical period: the commander of the 10th Special Forces Group, Colonel Othan "Shali" Shalikashville; General Frederick J. "Fritz" Kroesen of forces command, who controlled all units stationed in the United States; and the XVIII Airborne Corps chief of staff, Brigadier General James Lindsay. At one point during DELTA's shaky beginning, Shalikashville lined up all his senior commissioned and noncommissioned officers and told them flatly, "The job that Colonel Beckwith has to do is more important than the job we have to do. I would encourage anyone who has the desire to try out for this unit." When General Kingston's successor refused Beckwith's request to move DELTA into Bragg's underutilized post stockade, Lindsay saw to it that the unit would get it, reasoning, "Here we've got a nice stockade facility where we're keeping eleven bad guys. . . . Why don't we take the eleven and put them downtown in the Fayetteville jail? Your use of the stockade is better than the use it's being put to now. Colonel, you've got it!" Beckwith was obviously pleased that his problem had been solved so quickly. Ten years later, Lindsay donned eight stars on his shoulders and became commander of the newly created Special Operations Command responsible for providing combat-ready Special Operations Forces for rapid deployment to other unified commands around the world.

Still, support from the special operations community was not very strong at this point. Meticulously trained special forces units had conducted numerous missions during the Vietnam War, but now there wasn't a need for such specialists—or so the conventional leadership thought. And the conventional leadership controlled the Army and directed the downsizing of forces. Providentially, control of special forces fell to the commander of the JFK Special Warfare Center, and since General Kingston, his boss, was in control, Beckwith had the degree of freedom required to make DELTA a reality.

Sniper Rifles

Nearly all DELTA weapons—old or new—have been accurized to some degree by the unit's gunsmiths. Loose-fitting parts typically found even in quality mass-produced weapons are replaced by custom-built pieces with closer tolerances, specialized trigger mechanisms, and better sights. Before it was superseded by the heavy-barreled 40XB sniper rifle (specially manufactured for DELTA by Remington Arms), modifications were made to the trusty M14A1 to upgrade its already formidable performance as a sniper rifle.

Modifications typically include polishing and hand fitting the gas cylinder and piston to improve operation and reduce carbon buildup. Barrels are always carefully selected to

The Remington 7.62mm M40A1 sniping rifle mounting a ten-power U.S. Marine Corps telescope commonly used by DELTA.

The Springfield Armory 7.65mm M21 sniping system based on the M14 rifle.

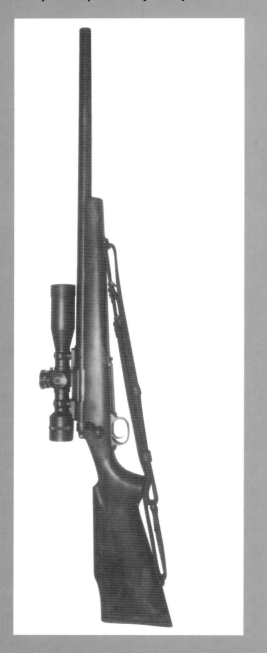

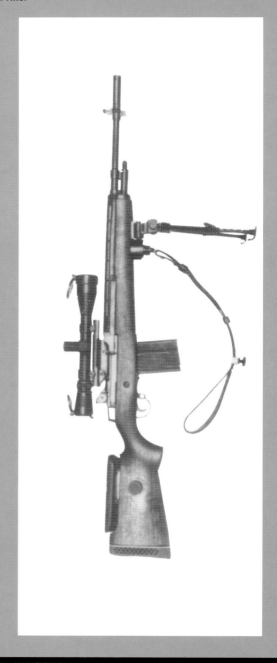

Snipers, with M24 weapons systems, prepare for operations in northern Afghanistan.

ensure correct specification tolerances and are bedded into the forearms with fiberglass compounds. Trigger housing groups are carefully fitted and polished to provide a crisp hammer release, and suppressors are fitted to eliminate sound and flash, which could reveal a sniper's position. Receivers can also be individually fitted to stocks using a fiberglass compound. The U.S. Army now purchases an off-the-shelf version of this weapon from the Springfield Armory called the M21 sniping rifle. DELTA troopers often use this weapon during training, and it also receives considerable reworking, such as having plastic spacers added to customize the length of the stock. The M40A1 and M24 sniping systems, standardized versions of the 40XB, are also used by the Army and Marines.

Complaints by the Rangers that DELTA would deepen their current manpower problems (partially true) and that the unit duplicated some of their functions (untrue) were brushed aside early on. Beckwith's only real opposition came from the commander of the 5th Special Forces Group at Bragg, Colonel Robert "Black Gloves" Montell, who believed that the shoot-from-the-hip hasty response was perfectly adequate.

About the time DELTA seemed to be a sure thing, Kingston was transferred to Korea, and Major General Jack "Bobo" Mackmull assumed command. No doubt Mackmull had received his marching orders from Washington to keep the program on track, but as a West Pointer and aviator, he

Assault Packs

Regular civilian backpacks were considered for situations when DELTA troopers had to move unnoticed through populated areas, but past experience had proven that commercial packs did not hold up to the rigors of special operations. The Eagle Industries A-III assault pack was found to exceed all special operations expectations and from a distance could easily pass as a civilian backpack.

was not very familiar with the missions and capabilities of this strange little unit under his command, and unfortunately, he made little effort to learn. Once DELTA was approved for activation, Mackmull was told to come up with a backfill unit until DELTA was certified for operations some two years in the future. Montell's 5th Special Forces Group received the nod.

To meet this requirement, Montell selected 40 special forces troopers and trained them in hasty-response techniques. Code-named *Blue Light*, the unit operated under the principle that a bird in the hand is worth two in the bush, and Mackmull approved both funding and personnel for the unit. Despite reassurances from insiders, it appears that Beckwith feared that Montell's stalwart professionals would derail DELTA before it had a chance to prove itself. If Beckwith lost his support in Washington, he would lose his unit.

Initially, what kept DELTA and its concept of a full-time, low-visibility CT organization alive was its strong supporters. When General Rogers discovered that expected resources were being routed away from DELTA, he went ballistic. From that point on, through the support from the chief of staff on down the line, DELTA was given the breathing room it needed to grow from a concept to a full-fledged force.

After 1st Special Forces Operational Detachment–DELTA was activated in October 1977, Beckwith had to select and train his new unit. DELTA troopers would have to blend perfectly into the civilian world when required and needed unique skills—from the military arts to climbing the sides of buildings to hot-wiring cars. Finally, on November 4, 1979, DELTA completed its certification exercises.

Clothing

From the early days of hasty-option operations, counterterrorist equipment has steadily evolved. Lightweight, highly rigid specialized clothing and equipment has now become standard for CT teams. Several European units such as the SAS and Germany's GSG-9 learned from experiences at the Iranian Embassy in London and at the Mogadishu airport that general-issue equipment is great for conventional forces but suffers from dangerous shortfalls when used during specialized operations. Much equipment development work has focused on the tactical assault vest and modular pouches attached to the upper torso and hips, which incorporate such items as extra ammo, radios, first-aid pouches, and rappelling rings. Despite the fact that the soldiers belong to teams, each man puts a great deal of faith in his individual gear. The equipment must be capable of accommodating a number of modifications to handle, for example, either flash/bang or gas grenades and either MP5 magazines or Colt 733 Commando magazines. Creating a basic vest capable of handling interchangeable sets of pouches and holders to adapt to each specific mission answered this need.

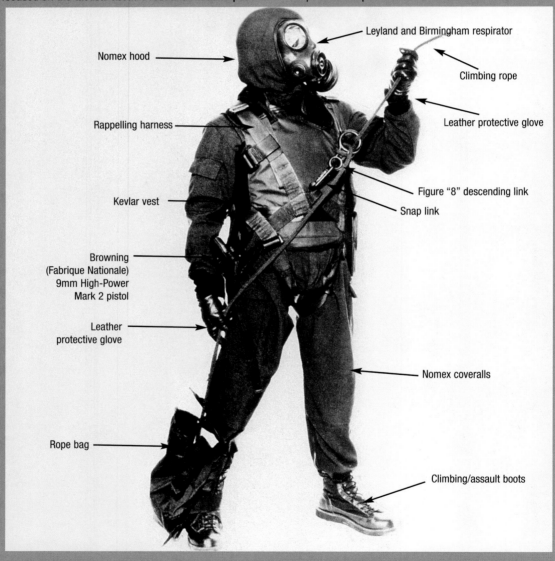

The figure-eight descending link not only prevents clothing from being dragged into the snap link but also allows the climber to control his descent with only one hand while leaving the other free to fire weapons, throw grenades, or place charges. This mountaineering device was added after the operation at the Iranian Embassy in London where an SAS commando was nearly killed by his own explosives. The soldier became stuck outside a window after a demolition had been placed and its fuse ignited. Only quick action by his buddies on the roof above saved his life.

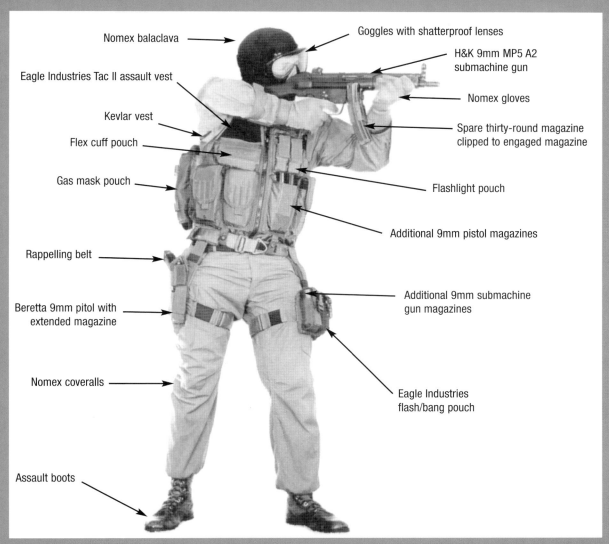

Nomex balaclava

Goggles with shatterproof lenses

H&K 9mm MP5 A2 submachine gun

Eagle Industries Tac II assault vest

Nomex gloves

Kevlar vest

Spare thirty-round magazine clipped to engaged magazine

Flex cuff pouch

Gas mask pouch

Flashlight pouch

Additional 9mm pistol magazines

Rappelling belt

Additional 9mm submachine gun magazines

Beretta 9mm pitol with extended magazine

Nomex coveralls

Eagle Industries flash/bang pouch

Assault boots

Delta troopers (and all CT specialists) wear mission-specific gear. While the man at above equipped for an average takedown, the SAS trooper at left is set to operate in a chemical environment and wears the minimum possible gear around his chest and hips to help ensure that nothing will snag his climbing rope.

A mixed group of special operators sporting upgraded Interceptor body armor, kneepads, and SATCOM prepare to move out in Afghanistan.

Chapter 3

THE MAKING OF A DELTA TROOPER

In the 82nd Airborne, I was better than any guy in my company. Over here I gotta hustle just to keep up.
—*A DELTA trooper*

Troopers delivered to a Navy submarine by an MH-60G Pave Hawk.

J oining a counterterrorist unit is similar to breaking into the big leagues of pro sports. But there are a few differences. Major league ball clubs have quite a few rookies on the squad, whereas CT units require veterans with basic special operations skills already refined to a razor's edge. And an error in the major leagues won't anyone's life.

CT units are composed of senior noncommissioned officers (NCOs) and several well-qualified officers. Continuous assignments in such units have not always been career enhancing, and despite the Army's recent elevation of special forces to full branch status, few officers stay around for more than one or two special forces tours. Those who do are usually *extremely* dedicated to their units, their troops, and the basic idea that the

worldwide terrorist threat and its network of supporters should be met head-on and eliminated. The men charged with carrying out low-visibility CT operations are chosen from a wide range of backgrounds. Each is selected based on his talents and the unit's specific needs.

Selection and Training

Special operations units—especially close-knit counterterrorist units—recruit in several ways. As with other occupations, word of mouth, networking, and personal recommendations are key. DELTA recruitment teams visit training centers, troop posts, and facilities such as the Command and General Staff College and NCO advance schools. These recruitment drives precede DELTA's fall and spring selection and assessment courses. Recruitment letters are also routinely mailed from Army personnel centers, and, as the unit's existence becomes more openly recognized, volunteers have been openly solicited in Army journals.

Soldiers are also individually recruited, based on a screening of their official records. Recruiters look for specific assets, such as language skills, key past assignments, military qualifications, or schools attended. From the compiled list of likely candidates, individuals are contacted and invited to volunteer.

DELTA's rigid entrance requirements are clearly spelled out for career officers and NCOs who may be enticed to leave their current postings for a new adventure. The pitch is always straightforward and unambiguous:

"ASSIGNMENT OPPORTUNITIES are available in the 1st Special Forces Operational Detachment–DELTA. DELTA is the Army's special operations unit that has been organized to conduct missions that combine rapid response with the surgical application of a wide variety of unique skills and the flexibility to maintain the lowest possible profile of U.S. involvement. . . . DELTA gives commissioned and noncommissioned officers unique opportunities for professional development. . . ."

Drawn from the active Army, Army reserve, and Army national guard, all DELTA members must pass a background investigation, be at least 22 years old, male, and a U.S. citizen. Each soldier's records are screened for psychological abnormalities and recurring discipline problems, and those accepting the challenge receive very thorough physical and eye examination. Commonly referred to as the Scuba/HALO physical, it is akin to the in-depth exams pilots receive.

After getting the thumbs up from the doctors, or "chancre mechanics," the prospective counterterrorist is subjected to a

Soldiers using the Stabo technique land on a Fort Bragg rooftop. Hanging free from the helicopter during their approach, the men land simultaneously instead of one at a time. The target area is framed with a 2x4 barrier in case any of the soldiers loses his footing.

All DELTA trainees are jump qualified, and previously acquired skills, such as scuba diving, are further refined during training. Troopers are assigned to specialized teams containing soldiers with the same skills, and many teams and elements are multidisciplined. A high-altitude, low-opening (HALO) team exits the rear of a C-141.

complete: a 40-yard inverted crawl in 25 seconds; 37 sit-ups in 1 minute; 33 pushups in 1 minute; a run, dodge, and jump course in 24 seconds; a 2-mile run in 16 minutes, 30 seconds; and a 100-meter swim while fully clothed and wearing boots.

Following the test, the candidates complete a speed march by traversing an 18-mile course as rapidly as possible. Since this is a psychological and a physical challenge, the passing times are never published. But many who have passed it agree that 10-minute miles are almost too slow!

Just like in the SAS course, the candidates have to show what they're really made of and are taken to one of several sites for a combination speed march, compass course, and survival exercise. These tests are now conducted on the rugged terrain of Camp Dawson, West Virginia, and a site has recently been added in the secured areas of Nellis Air Force Base, Nevada.

The Freedom to Fail or Succeed

If you were one of the few candidates to reach the 40-mile land navigation exercise, you'd find that the basic scenario goes like this: With all the ceremony of going off to a maximum-security prison, you and the other candidates are trucked out to the test site and dropped at separate starting points. As dawn breaks, you are given a set of instructions that amount to little more than a compass heading and a point on the map marking the final destination perhaps a half-dozen miles away. You are to select your route, and get there as quickly as possible.

Your thoughts run the gamut from, "What the hell am I doing here?" to "I hope I can pull this off." Even though you made some rough calculations at the start, you drop off to the side of the trail to ensure your initial calculations are correct. The map is hard to read, and harder to interpret, but you settle into the comfortable trot they taught you back at Bragg's Smoke Bomb Hill or Fort Benning. It starts to rain, but for the airborne, Ranger, or special forces type, rain is not a stranger. In most cases, the trial would be more enjoyable if you didn't remember that this was much more than just an exercise. You are here to show that you can hack whatever it takes to be part of DELTA.

As you navigate the trail, the shoulder straps of your 55-pound rucksack pinch and bind. Sweat trickles down your armpits, blurs your vision, and pools between your legs. After about 90 minutes, your experience from ranger school, the special forces qualification course, and numerous special forces

battery of tests to determine if he is psychologically sound. The cost of omitting extensive psychological tests was graphically displayed in Munich in 1972. At one point, the terrorists moved into the sights of the German sharpshooters, who then froze.

Approximately 100 prospective counterterrorists receive intensive physical testing every session, and high scores are an absolute requirement. DELTA's selection process closely follows the British SAS model, because those who helped set up the unit had worked closely with SAS special forces.

The candidate's ordeal begins with six grueling events that must be completed within the allotted time for a minimum of 60 points for each event. The candidates are, of course, expected to do better than the minimum. Volunteers are expected to

An instructor from the John F. Kennedy Special Warfare Center training group, exhausted after negotiating a demanding confidence course like DELTA's. He is indicative of the highly motivated, professional soldiers in the U.S. special operations community.

A trainee negotiates stairs to a room mock-up during entry-technique training at the special operations training (SOT) facility. The object is to engage the pop-up silhouette from uncomfortable angles while in motion.

group exercises takes over. So it's time to stop, review the situation, and drink some water. You look around the dense hardwoods and sense something in the underbrush near your left foot, and you slowly retreat a few steps as "Jake no shoulders" rattles a friendly greeting.

Moving down the trail, you get out of the drizzle, change your socks, and apply some Vaseline to your groin. You get your bearings and are off. Whether running the selection course in Appalachia, with its mountains, forests, and streams, or driving on in the Sierra Nevada wastelands, the expected results are the same. Just like General Forest, get there "firstest with the mostest." In your case, get there fastest—period.

You've been at this all day. The sun dipped below the wooded hills uncounted hours ago, and at each rendezvous you hope that

you'll be told to throw your ruck into the truck and get aboard. But for some bizarre reason, all you hear at each brief stop is the location of your next rendezvous. After about 12 hours of this, many volunteers rest too long or slow down so much that they can't beat the 20-hour time limit. Even good soldiers begin to look for excuses to quit, and many inevitably find them. But not you. Cold, wet, and numb with exhaustion, you move off again, continuing on until well after midnight, when you are unceremoniously informed that the exercise is over. The survivors rarely remember where they've been, how far they went, or how long it took.

By now, steady attrition has weeded the field down to a dozen or so. Many were cut because they couldn't meet the challenge, while others were sidetracked for other reasons, such as knee, ankle, and back injuries. The NCOs overseeing the

A trainee practices pistol shooting at multiple targets at one of the special operations training (SOT) facility's numerous ranges. Note the semi-crouch stance and two-handed pistol grip.

selection course steadfastly refuse to provide encouragement, and some soldiers drop out because they simply weren't mentally prepared to complete the course without the you-can-do-it encouragement that that was part of previous training. DELTA makes a great effort to ensure that those not selected know that they are *not* failures. Each dismissed candidate receives a certificate of training and is simply told that he wasn't selected.

The physical demands of the selection process are structured to put maximum psychological pressure on the candidates. A candidate must be able to use his physical, mental, and emotional strengths to his advantage. In the life-and-death reality of counterterrorism, you get only one chance to succeed. As Sun Tzu said, you have to know yourself as well as your enemy. If you are not ready to know what real fear is, to meet it head on and beat it, DELTA is not for you.

The trip back to Fort Bragg is surreal, and the exhausted candidates now have to face the final and, according to some, hardest part of the selection process: the interview, in which a board of DELTA veterans grills the survivors.

"So you're infiltrating an unfriendly area prior to taking down a terrorist hideout. Say you come across two little girls. You can't leave them. Do you take them along, tie them up, or kill them?"

"Tell us a little about Machiavelli."

"What were the arguments for and against our acquiring the Virgin Islands during World War I?"

"Was President Truman right or wrong to fire MacArthur?"

After four hours of this, some volunteers resemble frightened animals. The questions are serious, and serious answers are expected.

"Well, Sergeant, you've given a fine performance so far. Now tell us what you tend to blow it on."

"Why should we take you? What can you offer DELTA?"

"You're a good soldier!? So what!? Sergeant, we're up to our ears in good soldiers. Tell us about your unique skills, what you're really good at that's not military related."

In this tension-charged atmosphere, there are few right or wrong answers. The board is looking at the whole individual, including his values and how he handles himself under pressure.

An American counterterrorist team practices pistol shooting from several different positions. Ranges such as this one provide enclosed areas to practice room-clearing methods out of sight of prying eyes.

The objective is to find individuals who can both work with the team and yet operate independently without orders. In the end, only about 10 percent of the initial candidates make it into DELTA. Nevertheless, DELTA remains focused on the quality, not the quantity, of personnel entering the unit.

The SOT

The staff sergeant reports to Fort Bragg for some of the finest—and toughest—training in the world. He drives to the Special Operations Training (SOT) Facility, a multimillion-dollar complex built with support from Congress and the president for the war on terrorism in the early 1980s.

The SOT unfolds in the form of large two- and three-story buildings and training areas for heliborne insertions, and it's surprising that virtually anyone can get a look at this well-publicized facility.

The newcomer then passes the numerous open-aired and enclosed ranges where he'll train for the next two years. A thrill

rushes through him. This is going to be the ultimate adventure! He pulls up to the brick guardhouse, the guard compares his ID to the incoming roster for the day, and he's directed to park and await his escort.

Everything the trainee has seen so far speaks well of the command emphasis placed on the Army's counterterrorist mission, from the White House down through the major subordinate headquarters, the Joint Special Operations Command (JSOC). As DELTA's newest recruit waits for his escort, he is startled to see an MH-6 zoom overhead. Along each side is a trio of soldiers buckled into special side platforms for rapid egress. Just a moment later, the six commandos slip wearily from their Little Bird onto a helicopter pad near Lambert Road.

This specially modified Hughes chopper belongs to another important part of the team, the 160th Special Operations Aviation Regiment (Airborne), or SOAR. This unit is a result of the many problems experienced during *Desert I* and objectively outlined in its after-action review (AAR).

A counterterrorist operative demonstrates how to use a shotgun during a window entry.

Commonly referred to as the Holloway Report, the AAR pointed out that a major area to restructure, if future missions were to stand a chance, was helicopter operations, and the covert aviation unit was duly formed at Fort Campbell, Kentucky. Originally named Task Force 160, it soon became the major U.S. Army aviation support element for DELTA.

The commandos clearing the aircraft have darkened faces and wear a patrol, or ranger, cap. Clad in olive drab jungle fatigues and specially made vests and other web gear, they also carry rappelling gloves, snaplinks, and nonstandard Heckler & Koch MP5 submachine guns. As the SOAR 160 bird rises back into the sky, its stubby, rounded frame looks like an overweight bumblebee attempting to gain flight.

The facility's mission is to teach new methods and refine old skills in the art of counterterrorism. Some have referred to eliminating a terrorist situation as antiterrorism, but antiterrorism

refers to the skills and techniques used to help prevent terrorist attacks. Schools and courses teach basic antiterrorist methods and tactics, but the SOT addresses the final options of dealing with a terrorist incident that has already occurred. This is counterterrorism— DELTA's prime mission. Most CT operations require lightning-fast target-area entrances, which are intended to shock and disorient hostage takers. Carrying out such complicated maneuvers requires intensive training, teamwork, and mutual respect for everyone's abilities. These are the things new recruits will learn in DELTA's five-month operators' course.

Many will argue that specialized units for CT operations are too expensive. But even decades ago—well before the terrorist attacks of 9/11—it was obvious that a successful terrorist strike is devastating at multiple levels. Economic costs alone can top tens of millions of dollars, and priceless, innocent lives are put at risk or lost. The configuration of individual CT

A close-up of a "best-case" anchoring system, with abundant safety features. In the heat of a fast-paced takedown, such fine points often have to be bypassed.

An assault team conducts a forced entry. Lock picking is conducted with a charge of C4 plastic explosive.

units is decided by each country, but one piece of the equation remains firm: Counterterrorist skills are highly perishable and must be kept at razor's edge if teams hope to succeed. Appropriate training and constant study of the enemy's methods, personnel, and organization are an absolute necessity. The needed skills and support apparatus require substantial manpower and resources, but countries must be prepared to accept the costs, which are a pittance compared to the economic and human devastation wreaked by even one successful terrorist strike.

A CT operation has several distinct phases. First, the unit must get to the area of operations—hundreds or even thousands of miles away—by reliable, secure transportation. Simultaneously, immense amounts of intelligence must be collected, analyzed, and disseminated by supporting agencies. A critical issue at this phase is who is in charge. The Army's Special Operations Command (SOCOM) supports DELTA's training and related operational requirements, but, in time of crisis, JSOC bypasses the SOCOM link and directs the unit and the nation's other CT assets. Once deployed, the state department is the key decision-making element for foreign operations, while the justice department deals with problems within the United States. This simple chain of command allows a stovepipe of direction and support to the unit and cuts out a number of middlemen who would unintentionally hinder a mission's execution.

After arrival, the next phase is preparation. In its simplest form, target surveillance is begun; outer and inner security rings

If you can't go through the door or a window, go through the wall! Two U.S. operatives prepare to follow the blast into the next room.

are checked; command, control, and liaison functions are established; and incoming intelligence is analyzed. After all the players are satisfied (or the situation forces the issue), the next phase is the assault, or takedown, of the objective. Finally, swift withdrawal returns the force to its home base.

In this scenario, the new trooper is likely to fill a number of roles, and his titles may be many. As he progresses within the organization, he will use his past skills and experiences to benefit each team he is assigned to. For example, he may be a sniper because he went to sniper school while assigned to a ranger battalion. If his demolitions background is good, he may work with some very exotic toys designed to blow off the smallest locks or take down the entire wall of a room with minimal disturbance to occupants in the next room. As a door-kicker or shooter, his skills will be fine-tuned in the art of lockpicking, room entry, and target identification.

The SOT teaches troopers various methods of entry, seizure, and exit. They learn to rappel into second- and third-story windows to reach terrorists and their victims, and how to

kick open a door, use stun grenades to disorient the terrorists, and then closely follow the blast into the room. Each member of a four-man team must know not only where he is going, but also precisely where his teammates will be and in what direction their fields of fire are directed.

In the closely orchestrated ballet of death known as close-quarters battle (CQB), the troopers learn to pick their targets quickly and then instantly place a minimum of two shots in an eye socket–sized kill zone from as far as 50 feet away. This technique is known as the double tap. Moving quickly through the area, the team secures everyone with plastic flex cuffs and leaves the sorting out and medical treatment to the follow-on police forces.

This is the type of assault that most people associate with counterterrorist forces. During a takedown, terrorists and hostages alike see only dark apparitions entering behind the stun or flash/bang of grenades. Every trooper is completely clad in sophisticated armor. Heads are protected by Kevlar helmets identical to current military issue. Under this Fritz helmet is a flame-resistant Nomex balaclava. An earphone and/or micro-

"Walk-throughs" of room-clearing operations are run with troopers wearing progressively more equipment so the men will gain a clear idea of how different combinations of gear restrict vision and movement. They must attain extreme levels of proficiency—including expertise with personal weapons—while wearing a variety of equipment combinations. Troopers in coveralls prepare to enter a special operations training (SOT) facility "killing house" **Opposite:** to perform their ballet of death. Note the mannequin terrorists and hostage in closet.

phone provides instant tactical communications. Everyone involved in the decision-making process and execution must be provided with real-time information in order to control the unfolding operation.

Depending on the situation, a trooper may also wear eye protection in the form of shatterproof goggles or a protective chemical mask. His upper torso is encased in a Kevlar vest, for gunshot and blast fragmentation protection, over a dark Nomex coverall or tactical battle dress. Over this, a variety of general equipment is worn, along with items that will support his specific tasks. Some troopers will have ammunition and myriad survival aids, such as powerful miniature flashlights and radio receivers. Others will have a variety of grenades, ammo, knives, and first-aid equipment. When medical assistance is not immediately available, CT teams carry a medical pouch containing assorted dressings, IV tubing, saline solutions, and tourniquets.

Individual weapons are dictated by each situation. Everyone has a favorite, but training on all available CT weapons is required. Most room entries begin with the lead man using a submachine gun or a semiautomatic pistol. To expedite door-kicking procedures, shotguns fire a sabot or lead slug to blow off the barrier's hinges. Many insist that a submachine gun or a shotgun, which can be carried in one hand, is the ideal weapon, and some even mount laser pointers or mini flashlights on their weapons for operations in dimly lit conditions. Plenty of ammo is always strategically placed.

Regardless of equipment, each man is aware that one lucky shot or well-placed booby trap can ruin the best-laid plans. From the soles of his Gore-Tex assault boots to the crown of his Kevlar helmet, the DELTA trooper's equipment is constantly reviewed and updated.

Training generally falls into two categories. First the FNG (f—ing new guy) will go through individual skills training

Two special operators aboard an MH-53M prepare to conduct a water drop.

supplied by the major carriers at various sites around the country.

Additional CT training teaches infiltration methods for moving into isolated target areas. These include high-altitude, low-opening (HALO) or high-altitude, high-opening (HAHO) parachuting, underwater rescue operations using scuba techniques and miniature submersible vehicles for long-distance travel, and rappelling and fast-roping from helicopters. Teams may also learn techniques for driving various all-terrain vehicles.

Upon completion, the FNG is assigned to a team, and honing his new skills begins in his troop. Regular cross-training occurs with related foreign and domestic CT units, such as Britain's SAS or our own Navy SEAL (Sea-Air-Land) teams. Some DELTA troopers will also find themselves temporarily assigned to personal protection duty, providing security to key U.S. personnel, such as ambassadors in Central America and the Middle East.

The Killing House

"Take a break, you heroes." The team sergeant chuckles to himself every time he uses that line. If everything goes as it should, his jibe would either cause a rush of catcalls or a deep-throated moan from the assembled trainees. This time, the muted response indicates that the humid North Carolina weather is sapping the team's strength. More importantly, it was a good indicator of what they should do for the rest of the day. The team sergeant adjusts the training schedule and walks through a room-clearing exercise without the required live ammunition. Training accidents are acceptable but are not sought after.

Fifty meters to the west, a second and much more experienced team just finished with its own room-clearing exercise, and the men are given one of the most beloved commands in the military lexicon: "Take a break."

It's a 30-minute break, but the team members think it should be longer. Sprawled under the pines, each trooper tries to find a comfortable position while trying to keep his equip-

designed to break conventional army habits, such as not shooting outside of prescribed safety limits, and much emphasis is placed on individual action and initiative. New habits are instilled in the FNG, such as the double tap, used when a pumped-up terrorist in the midst of a takedown cannot be talked into surrendering.

Once this basic training is completed, the FNG enters the team training phase where he's taught how to handle himself in close-quarters battle whether in a building, on a train, or on an aircraft. For example, the trooper will be given his first taste of an aircraft takedown in a large mockup of a civilian passenger jet at the SOT before training on a variety of actual aircraft

Opposite page: "Hang on!" A search-and-rescue para-jumper, or "PJ," of an Air Force special tactics squadron is hoisted along with his patient out of a secure landing zone.

The business end of a special operations soldier's 5.56mm M4 with all the bells and whistles. Note the tactical vest, body armor, and blood type attached to his left sleeve.

ment away from the grit and sand. Rivulets of sweat trickle down grimy faces as Nomex gloves are removed and calloused hands brush the sweat away from bloodshot eyes. Each man wears an assault suit of black Nomex, and some already removed their Kevlar helmets and flashproof balaclavas. Goggles, used to protect against flying debris, lie in the crown of the helmet, along with sweat-soaked gloves and face masks. The team members take care to switch off individual communications earpieces and microphones.

Each trooper wears body armor to protect his throat and chest and armored shorts to protect his vulnerable groin area. Some troopers add knee and elbow pads under their assault suits, and some wear shin protectors to avoid bruises and cut shins from the furniture-cluttered killing house. Troopers are equipped with either a special-purpose Mossberg automatic shotgun or a 9mm Heckler & Koch MP5 submachine gun.

Most of the free world's CT forces swear by this weapon, and some argue that it's the best German export since fräuleins, Mercedes-Benzes, and beer. The sniper teams on this exercise are also equipped with M24 sniper rifles. Though there are more advanced systems, the accurized Remington 700 bolt-action rifle with five-round fluted, detachable magazine is still the favorite. Its stainless-steel barrel and hefty .300 Winchester Magnum round provide the power required to reach out and touch someone. All members of the sweeper team carry the 9mm Beretta Model 92F pistol, the standard sidearm of the U.S. Army.

While some troopers smoke and joke over the break, others chug nourishing liquids from canteens and jugs. Like each man's love for his personal weapon, each also enjoys anything liquid, including Gatorade, spring water, juice, or plain tap water. Unlike Hollywood's image, hard-drinking troopers are not the norm.

At the end of the break, the team sergeant growls, "Saddle up, you assholes." Staff Sergeant Dawkins hated it when the sergeant major used his hard John Wayne voice, and comments sarcastically, "I really wonder if John Wayne ever called anyone an asshole." Troopers grumble as they rise to their feet and adjust their equipment. Gathering around the team leader, Sergeant Major Greg Tusconey, the men fall into a loose formation facing their boss.

Looking up from his notebook, Sergeant Major Tusconey begins with an in-depth critique of the morning's exercise. He cites their strengths as well as their weaknesses. When finished, he faces his soldiers and says in a matter-of-fact tone, "OK, girls, let's get our shit together and try it again." The resounding reply to being called girls is indicative of a team that can give as much as it can take.

Returning to their briefing area, the team members arrange themselves on wooden benches placed in front of a graphic representation of the rooms in the killing house. A key factor in these exercises, as well as in actual assaults, is the need for accurate and up-to-date information about the physical layout of the operation site, as well as the locations of the hostages and their terrorist keepers. Stepping in front of the diagram, the sergeant major describes the mission for the team in clear, concise, and pointed terms:

"At 1730 hours last night, terrorists assaulted the U.S. Embassy and took 16 state department employees as hostages. Two U.S. Marines were killed during the initial assault. We are to prepare for a deliberate takedown of the building on order from higher." Stopping to scan the team for questions, he continues. "Outer security has been established by the local police, and inner security has been established by the hasty response team from the 10th Special Forces Group until after we arrive and take over responsibility for the mission. Recon of the building has been conducted, along with a debrief of our people and the locals who have solid, current intel."

Tusconey proceeds to outline the rehearsal schedules and timetables and how he envisions the takedown. After the briefing is completed, troopers are quizzed and then individual and team rehearsals are begun. As the last rays of the fading sun are engulfed by the approach of a cool, wet front, the final preparations are completed. For this exercise, chopper support will come from the 160th SOAR.

The team is divided into sniper and assault elements to coordinate the operation's precise timing. The two sniper teams each consist of a spotter and a shooter. They are linked with the assault team, sweeper team, and command center by radio. Each sniper team moves along individual routes previously reconned and takes positions offering vantage points overlooking the target area. The assault element, meanwhile, moves toward their pickup zone (PZ) to rendezvous with an inbound chopper. Word circulates that the order has been received. The mission is on.

Because this is night operation, infrared reflective tape is applied around each member's chest, wrists, ankles, helmet, and equipment. Using AN/PVS-7 night-vision goggles (NVGs), all assault members will be easily seen in the heat of night combat. The team divides evenly and prepares to board the chopper. Like a giant dragonfly, the MH-60 Pave Hawk glides into the PZ, where the team immediately loads through the side doors. The pilot's eyes are unaided but his copilot wears aviator's AN/AVS-6 NVGs. Immediately, the team leader places the spare set of headphones over his ears and communicates with the pilot.

"Evening," says the pilot in a slow, Southern drawl.

"How's it going?" replies the sergeant major.

Formalities exhausted, Tusconey quickly briefs the aircrew on how the team will carry out the infil as the aircraft nears the target. Due to the lousy weather, the landing zone (LZ) will be the building's sloping rooftop, and the team will drop onto a very small area at its peak, where a flat space has been located during photo recon analysis. Normally, the team would rappel or fast-rope in, but the wet weather and reduced visibility give them an added advantage and they'll be able to get closer to the target. With clockwork precision, the Pave Hawk angles into the rooftop LZ and flares out level and steady. Looking through his NVGs, Tusconey sees that everyone is ready, and in a low, distinct voice says, "Stand by, stand by." Prompted by his warning, the sniper teams report in: "Sniper One, ready. Target sighted." "Sniper Two ready. No target." At his hand signal, the lead team members prepare to exit. Taking a deep breath, he gives the command, "Go!"

The soldiers leap onto the mist-shrouded roof and fan out across its tricky incline in a predetermined (and well-rehearsed) pattern. Almost as quickly as the bird arrived at the LZ, it disappears into the night. Two team members attach green nylon climbing ropes to anchor points, drop them over the sides of the building along predetermined entry sites, and kneel in anticipation after attaching their snaplinks. Six other men move to a rooftop door and, after determining that it's locked, move into a tight file along the outside wall. The door hinges will have to be shot off.

Ten seconds since the team landed: At the command, "Go!" the number one man, armed with a Mossberg 12-gauge

After entry, the team fans out along the walls before picking targets.

shotgun, blasts the offending hinges off the wooden door. Yanking the door to the side, the number two trooper rapidly steps into the doorway, where he immediately places his back to the dimly lit stairwell wall. Sweeping the staircase with his NVG, he alerts follow-on troopers to the situation he is observing. Number three now bursts through the doorway and, in calculated steps, moves down the stairs and secures the top-floor stairwell. Peering down the hallway, he clearly and rapidly speaks into his microphone: "Number three, hallway clear." Trooper number four is immediately at his side, having followed his partner down the stairs. As number three moves to the right, number four moves left and blends into the darkened hallway. Both troopers' H&Ks move in measured arcs: ceiling to floor, left to right. Whenever a trooper's eyes move under his NVG, the stubby barrel of his MP5 follows, ready to spit out a lethal three-round burst along that same visual arc.

The second assault element of four men moves along the right side of the hallway toward a door on the right. The lead man (number three) senses motion in the room. Reaching down along his left thigh, he extracts a pop can-sized flash/bang grenade from his leg pouch. Bringing it up to his right hand, which still clutches an MP5, he slides the grenade's pullring over his gloved thumb. While holding the safety spoon, he pulls the ring. Gently rolling the grenade into the room, he flattens himself against the wall as he warns his teammates. "Grenade" reverberates through the soldiers' earphones and, almost immediately, "Go!" is commanded before the nonlethal grenade has expended its package.

Number five slides into the left side of the doorway as the room erupts in multiple flashes and explosions designed to disrupt, disorient, and illuminate. As he moves through the door, number six follows and slides into the smoke-filled room along the doorway's right wall. He is followed by numbers seven and eight, who had entered the floor through windows on the other side of the building. Number seven backs number five by taking on any targets from his twelve- through three-o'clock (the right hand wall). Number five already has acquired a target through his NVG in his twelve- through nine-o'clock area along the left wall.

A masked terrorist is wildly trying to bring his AK47 assault rifle to bear on a young woman strapped to a chair near the center of the office. Number five squeezes a three-round burst into the throat of the terrorist, who goes down in a spasmatic heap.

As number seven checks the terrorist for other weapons and vital signs, number five maintains a steady aim on the lifeless corpse. Flipping the terrorist over on his stomach, number seven expertly pins his wrists together with flex cuffs. After a quick check of the room, numbers six and eight now check the bound female for booby traps. More than one rescue has ended in disaster when the rescuers failed to check for explosives secreted somewhere on a hostage. A grenade or stick of dynamite can turn a rescue into a tragedy. After the check is completed, the team exits the room. Eight seconds have passed. As the leader leaves, he announces, "Number two, one terrorist down, one hostage secured, main room, top floor" to the command post and other team members. Now it's up to the sweepers and backup police forces to take charge of the room.

This process will continue until the "embassy" is cleared of terrorists and all the hostages are accounted for. After the team exits the building, they move to an assembly area and are whisked away for an in-depth debriefing. If this had been a real takedown, actual terrorists and hostages would be considerably more unpredictable than the mannequins and pop-up targets the team had to deal with. Local police, medical personnel, and the sweepers would have also been moving simultaneously through the building to deal with the carnage left behind and make a complete record of what happened.

During such exercises, the trooper is trained not to act like Rambo: Never fire from the hip and always extend your folding stock. Fire at close range and don't waste ammo. You learn how to move: Dropping to a crouch, firing, dropping and firing again, and moving to the next position. You learn to move quickly through doorways and get in position and maintain proper trigger control.

Chapter 4

DECADE OF FRUSTRATION

General [Bernard] Rogers told me of a note from the president. It had surfaced in the tank earlier in the day [October 18, 1977] and asked, "Do we have the same capability as the West Germans?" Much discussion ensued before it was decided that we did not. One of the generals present had said, "Well I'm not going over to the White House to tell him we don't."
—Colonel Charlie A. Beckwith, U.S. Army (Retired)

A U.S. flag burns on the Rhein-Main Air Base perimeter fence during a period of mass left-wing demonstrations and terrorist strikes against American targets in Germany.

Throughout the 1980s, DELTA faced a number of events that might have caused lesser organizations to collapse. The troopers trained hard but were seldom deployed. They watched helplessly as Americans were whisked from streets and university offices in Beirut and seized in large groups in hijacked airliners and

ships. Worse yet, the men geared up for numerous rescue operations that were canceled. During this time, the unit also received a disturbing amount of unwanted publicity. In addition to a highly publicized financial scandal involving DELTA members, easy access to the Special Operations Training Facility (SOT) may have been a factor in the media's knowledge of deployments during several hostage crises.

Although it's shocking to think that a unit on the cutting edge of America's war on terrorism was—and still is, in appearance at least—so vulnerable, it was only one factor among many that plagued counterterrorism. In addition to the security problems associated with CT operations, interdepartmental squabbles and convoluted command-and-control issues abounded. For example, the FBI is responsible for handling terrorist incidents at home, yet DELTA has to supply badly needed backup. The 1986 Statue of Liberty Centennial in New York City and the 1984 Olympics in Los Angeles, in spite of numerous jurisdictional and legal problems, provided the models for DELTA's continuing assistance at major domestic events.

When overseas CT operations are planned, numerous diplomatic issues become critical, and the state department steps to the forefront. A most basic question that must be asked before contemplating foreign operations is: What sovereign nation wants to relinquish command and control to United States military forces conducting such highly visible operations on their soil? No matter how discreetly DELTA may conduct itself in the run-up to an operation, every hostage rescue is a high-visibility operation *after* its well-publicized conclusion. The implication for the nation hosting DELTA is that it doesn't have the resources to take care of its own internal problems, which can have significant domestic, international, and political ramifications. Add to this mess the fact that

A DELTA trooper gives a German counterterrorist a hand before he disappears over the edge.

the Joint Special Operations Command, the direct link between DELTA and the president (known as the National Command Authority) and the Joint Chiefs of Staff (JCS), can receive marching orders from both. The JCS is better qualified to oversee operations involving DELTA, but common sense remains a missing ingredient, as can be seen by the less-than-desirable results in Grenada.

Operation Honey Badger—Aftermath

The fallout from the inferno of *Desert I* was complicated and far reaching. Not only did President Jimmy Carter lose his bid for re-election, but Egypt's supportive president, Anwar Sadat (who was already on a number of hit lists for his part in the Camp David Accords), was now a principal target of Iranian-sponsored fanatics for allowing the Great Satan to launch Operation *Eagle Claw* from his country. Sadat would soon die at the hands of Muslim fundamentalists.

JCS planners continued their work, and soon a new mission to rescue the hostages in Iran, code-named *Honey Badger*, was put together under the direction of the renowned and much-respected General Richard Secord. Armed with the proper special operations support—and the hard-learned lessons from *Eagle Claw*—he assembled a powerful force of special operations aviators, special forces and DELTA troopers, intelligence collectors, and agents who were prepared to go it again. But it was not meant to be. On January 19, 1981, some two minutes after Ronald Reagan was sworn in as President of the United States, the hostages were released.

One of the more interesting aspects to emerge from planning and coordinating for Operation *Honey Badger* was the structuring of special operations aviation and intelligence support. Task Force 160 emerged as a special operations aviation unit that would gain international fame in the 1990s and early 2000s. The intelligence requirements were already in place with

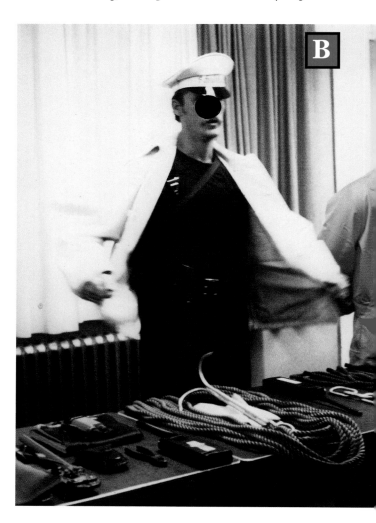

Counterterrorist specialists must be able to use any ruse or disguise to get close to hostage-holding sites, such as aircraft or buildings. Here, U.S. Army counterterrorist operatives display equipment and disguises during a briefing for General Bernard Rogers, supreme allied commander, Europe, in the early 1980s. (A) One of the typical "European businessmen" holsters his 9mm Beretta pistol and (B) a "street cleaner," standing beside a "municipal worker," shows off his protective vest and ammunition belt. Note the equipment on display.

a unit known as the FOG. The Foreign Operating Group was a special operations unit initially formed to deal with U.S. Embassy force protection issues. The CIA was unable to support DELTA operators, and in order to support future operations, the Pentagon saw FOG as a solution to the need for signals and human intelligence (SIGINT and HUMINT), as well as personal security problems. The unit was redesignated as the Intelligence Support Activity (ISA).

To help dampen the firestorm of criticism that erupted after *Desert I*, a six-officer review group was appointed by the chairman of the JCS, General David C. Jones. It was chaired by Admiral James L. Holloway, and the balance of its membership consisted of generals from the Army, Air Force, and Marines with experience in either special or clandestine operations.

The investigators concluded that *Eagle Claw* was plagued by untested operational methods, poor communications procedures, and a dangerously informal command structure lacking unity of command. Training for the mission, moreover, had been conducted by its various components at different sites without a full dress rehearsal using all the assigned elements—something that would have highlighted the most glaring operational and equipment shortfalls. The commission recommended that "a permanent field agency" of the JCS be established with "assigned staff personnel and certain assigned forces" and that a "murder board" of military experts be formed to independently examine mission plans before execution.

As for Colonel Beckwith, he was asked by General Meyer to formalize an earlier proposal for a permanently operating joint task force that would fall directly under the JCS and combine dedicated Army, Navy, and Air Force elements during its training and planning. Beckwith and others had long voiced the opinion that this type of organization was needed, and Major General John Singlaub put it best when he stated that *Eagle Claw* didn't work because, "We tried to bring disparate units from all over the armed forces—from all over the world—and then put them into an ad hoc arrangement to do a very complicated plan."

Beckwith's proposal to establish a Joint Special Operations Command (JSOC) was approved by Meyer in May 1980, and Beckwith was soon transferred from DELTA to the newly formed, independent organization he helped create. He missed the excitement of leading a combat team, though, and remarked that his staff billet "ain't as good a job [as DELTA]." Beckwith retired in 1981.

DELTA's friends in high places went to even higher places, and the post-Beckwith organization thrived. The unit, with about 100 men making up two small squadrons plus support before *Eagle Claw*, grew to a relatively stable force of 300 during the early 1980s—enough for three full-sized squadrons. The unit also benefited greatly from the new *Tasks, Conditions and Standards for DELTA*, or the Black Book, which was produced only because General Meyer forced Beckwith to compose it.

Meyer, now the Army's chief of staff, was anxious that DELTA not reinvent the wheel with each new commander and wanted it to retain its SAS-type structure, one that is unique within the Army. Four troops of approximately 16 men make up a squadron, with each troop able to reconfigure itself into eight-, six-, four-, three-, or two-soldier teams or elements. This degree of flexibility is key to DELTA's ability to handle virtually any terrorist scenario.

DELTA also moved its headquarters from the old post stockade to the new state-of-the-art SOT, nicknamed "Wally World." But it wasn't just DELTA that came up a big winner from the increased awareness of the terrorist threat. The whole military benefited as the obvious candidate to receive new funds. And the funds did flow: to Air Force special operations, Navy SEALS, Army aviation, Rangers, and special forces, as well as a large supporting cast in the various services, such as the Army's Intelligence Support Activity (ISA).

The state department, however, would soon emerge as the biggest winner. Being in the best position to judge the political ramifications of U.S. actions on a host nation's territory, it received the responsibility for overseeing all overseas counterterrorist operations. But though the United States now had a well-organized CT apparatus in place, the future would not be rosy.

Operation *Urgent Fury*

After Ronald Reagan became president in 1981, he "let it be known to friend and foe alike" that he had learned from the hard lessons of his predecessors. Surrounded by capable and, in some cases, hawkish advisors, Reagan was determined that, like the sheriffs of the Old West, he would clean up the world and make it safe for women and children. All he needed was a place to start and the force to sweep up the mess. He didn't have long to wait. At the southern end of the Antilles chain lies the beautiful Caribbean island of Grenada. A former ward of the British Empire, this idyllic 8- by 15-mile island was to be the testing ground for the new president and the changes that had been made in the special operations community since *Desert I*.

On October 19, 1983, Grenada's Marxist prime minister, Maurice Bishop, and several cabinet members were executed by

Above: U.S. and GSG-9 counterterrorists conducting joint training at a West German site. A classic procedure in building clearing is for a team to rappel to a roof from a helicopter, then work its way from top to bottom, outside to inside. Such operations require split-second timing and in-depth coordination. Note that this special ops UH-1N Huey, though painted black for night operations, is clearly marked as an American military helicopter for any German operatives taking part in a joint takedown.

Right: After rappeling down the building side, a U.S. operative prepares to enter a window. His teammate has already successfully completed this tricky maneuver. During actual operations, there is always the risk that an unexpected greeting awaits the team.

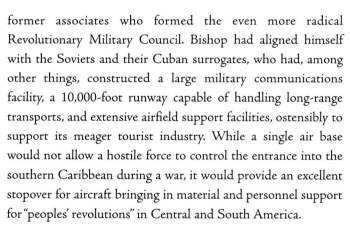

former associates who formed the even more radical Revolutionary Military Council. Bishop had aligned himself with the Soviets and their Cuban surrogates, who had, among other things, constructed a large military communications facility, a 10,000-foot runway capable of handling long-range transports, and extensive airfield support facilities, ostensibly to support its meager tourist industry. While a single air base would not allow a hostile force to control the entrance into the southern Caribbean during a war, it would provide an excellent stopover for aircraft bringing in material and personnel support for "peoples' revolutions" in Central and South America.

With the execution of the genuinely popular leader, widespread protests broke out on the island and, when the military opened fire on the demonstrators, the die was cast. The threat to the region caused an uproar among the neighboring Caribbean nations, and the Reagan administration believed that a radical Marxist government that thought nothing of shooting its own citizens would, sooner or later, use the 600 American students at the island's medical school as pawns in a dangerous

game to keep the U.S. military from closing down the airfield. This was a hostage situation waiting to happen, so the United States moved quickly to launch Operation *Urgent Fury*.

Special operations elements had a primary mission to secure and protect U.S. and allied citizens from hostile Grenadian and Cuban forces. The secondary mission was to assist in the airfield seizure, which would expedite the arrival of follow-on forces. Leading the assaults were several of the U.S. military's elite and (until then) classified units. UH-60 Black Hawks of Task Force 160 flew directly from the United States to a nearby island launch site with the help of additional internal fuel tanks, while MH-6s were brought in by Air Force cargo planes. During the early morning hours of October 25, the expert aviators of Task Force 160 ferried their ground counterparts, DELTA, to targets near the airfield at Point Salines, where they were to carry out a direct-action mission ahead of two ranger battalions parachuting in at dawn. Their target was the airfield control facilities which, it turned out, were heavily ringed by misplaced, but marginally effective, automatic weapons. A second mission entailed the takedown of Fort Rupert and Richmond Hill Prison, where DELTA participated in the assault to free selected Grenadians and any U.S. citizens being held as a result of the coup d'etat. One Black Hawk was lost to Soviet-made ZSU-23-2 (twin 23mm) antiaircraft guns. Men and aircraft were lost and some figures are still classified. The lack of timely, on-the-spot intelligence had again reared its ugly head.

Several members of the elite Navy SEAL Team Six have privately related that they had an especially rough time as DELTA and the Task Force 160 units were running into their own problems in the south. One deadly incident occurred when four SEAL team members parachuted into rough seas to conduct a linkup with a surface vessel that was to take them in close for a water infiltration. The drowning of these four men didn't stop the mission, but it tragically demonstrated that even the best sometimes cannot overcome the odds.

A major concern was the safety of the British government's representative. Tasked to keep him from being captured by the Revolutionary Armed Forces, 22 other members of SEAL Team Six flew in by chopper, fast-roped onto the rooftop and grounds of the governor's residence, and took control. A stunned Grenadian defense unit summoned help from two Soviet-supplied BTR-60 armored personnel carriers mounting multiple machine guns. The sudden appearance of substantial hostile elements hastily ended the evacuation of Government House. With neither antiarmor weapons nor good communications, the team held out as best they could until a Specter gunship came to their rescue. But even with the help of the AC-130's massive firepower, up to half of the rescue party is reported to have been wounded by the time Marines reached them.

Months later, a veteran SEAL discussed the operation, "Thank God it was just the Grenadians. Every time some nonqualified son of a bitch plans or directs our operations, we get our asses handed to us on a silver platter. It just ain't right." The end result of *Urgent Fury* was that closer control over special operations planning would, at least for a while, be handled by thoroughly qualified people.

Although the Army refused to either confirm or deny the use of Special Operations Forces for nearly eight years, ABC News was able to extract a concession that one Task Force 160 captain was killed and 11 DELTA troopers were injured after broadcasting footage of the downing of a Black Hawk—an event previously unaccounted for in the Pentagon recap of the operation. An American resident of Grenada had shot the film; other footage showed MH-6s, aircraft for which no procurement information had been publicly released. ABC News identified them as Hughes 500 helicopters, their civilian designation.

After the operation, increasingly bitter complaints over the secrecy surrounding special operations were heard from some quarters of the media. There was also the dubious claim that only the American public was being denied access to information, since the Soviets supposedly already knew about such activities. While this will continue to be a subject for debate, even relatively low losses can have a severe impact on a small unit's capabilities. And if the small unit performs a mission of vital strategic importance, that loss may be magnified a hundred-fold. Not only do Western intelligence agencies monitor terrorist networks, but the terrorists themselves monitor CT organizations, with the assistance of friendly governments that track Western units and capabilities through press reports and espionage. It is not in the best interests of the United States to reveal losses in key covert units within days—or even months—of their occurrence. In this case, freedom of information must take a back seat to security.

Trouble in the Mediterranean

On the heels of *Urgent Fury*, members of the Italian terrorist Red Brigade abducted U.S. General James L. Dozier from his apartment on December 17, 1982. Authorities would later learn that Dozier was not the intended victim; a Navy admiral had been the group's actual target. Regardless of who was snatched, the impact throughout Europe was the same— virtually ever senior officer viewed himself or his family as a prime terrorist target.

Against this background of confusion, experts from various special operations units converged on Italy. To their credit, the Italians told everyone to kindly go home since this was their turf. But while all door-kickers were sent packing, they did keep some special operators who could assist with such exotic needs as radio and telephone intercept.

With the help of U.S. signal-intercept personnel, the Italians located and rescued the kidnapped general, and American CT "experts" learned one more lesson about dealing with the real world.

In 1982, Iran sent roughly 2,000 fanatical Revolutionary Guards to the Lebanese free-for-all civil war as "volunteers." While many of them would perish in regular combat against Christian militiamen (and leftist Shiites, Druz militiamen, renegade Palestinians, U.S. Marine snipers, and Israeli, Lebanese, and Syrian soldiers), a select few would meet their

The U.S. Marine Corps barracks, Beirut, Lebanon, seconds after a suicide bomber detonated an explosives-filled truck. Lebanese rescue workers and U.S. Marines search through the flattened barracks. The terrorist drove directly past Marine guards who had been ordered not to carry loaded weapons. There were lessons to be learned: Listen to the warnings of counterterrorist specialists, and shoot first and worry about CNN later.

The television image of a TWA pilot being prevented from talking with reporters by an armed hijacker at Beirut airport in June 1985.

fate in a less conventional manner. These "martyrs" drove explosive-laden trucks into barracks, embassies, and other high-priority targets. On the night of April 18, 1983, 40 French paratroopers and 241 U.S. Marines were killed by a pair of these truck bombers after failing to heed the lessons of a similar attack on a U.S. Embassy building earlier that year.

Another incident in late October 1983 involved members of the 10th Special Forces Group who were billeted in a downtown hotel while training and advising the Lebanese army. The group's commander, Colonel Richard Potter, was warned that the group's quarters were targeted for yet another suicide bombing. Potter, DELTA's former deputy commander and a veteran of *Desert I*, was not about to let such warnings go unheeded and immediately moved his force to a Lebanese army base north of the city.

On December 4, 1984, DELTA was sent to assault a Kuwaiti airliner hijacked on its way to Pakistan. Two American passengers were killed during the incident, and the aircraft was forced to fly to Iran, where the terrorists and hostages were released before the unit could intervene. Six months later, on June 14, the unit returned to the region for an assault on TWA Flight 847, but the affair ended before they could be employed; one off-duty Navy serviceman on board was murdered. DELTA failed to come to grips with terrorists again during the *Achille Lauro* affair in October, and the resulting fiasco at Sigonella Naval Air Station, Sicily, again illustrated that the Italians zealously maintained jurisdiction on their own turf.

The Palestinian extremists who commandeered the *Achille Lauro* had been persuaded to leave it at Alexandria, Egypt, in return for safe conduct to friendly Tunisia, where the PLO maintained its headquarters. They left Egypt by commercial passenger jet immediately ahead of DELTA's arrival, but the jet was quickly intercepted by U.S. F-14 Tomcat fighters, which diverted it to the U.S.–Italian air base. Once the airliner was forced to land, it was quickly surrounded by Navy SEALs, who were, in turn, surrounded by Italian *carabonari*, who also blocked their C-141 with security vehicles. Since both groups were attempting to carry

Rotary- and Fixed-Wing Assets

The Holloway Report on Operation Eagle Claw laid bare the grievous deficiencies in special operations aviation that contributed to the disaster at Desert I, and chief among them was the lack of interoperability between the armed services. The conglomeration of hardware fielded by special operations aviation was the most visible manifestation of this shortcoming.

Throughout the early 1980s, special operations aviation soldiered on with an unwieldy mix of helicopters. Depending on the mission (and what was available), a DELTA trooper might find himself working with CH-3 Jolly Green Giants, CH-53C Sea Stallions, UH-1N Twin Hueys, CH-47D Chinooks, some newer (and extensively modified) UH-60A Black Hawks, HH-53B and C Pave Low IIIs, and substantially upgraded versions of the OH-6A Cayuse called AH-6 and MH-6 Little Birds. One highly capable

helicopter that DELTA could not count on using, except, perhaps, in the most extreme emergency, was the RH-53D of Eagle Claw. The Navy's entire fleet of this countermine version of the Sea Stallion amounted to only 24 aircraft before a half dozen were lost in the Dasht-e Kavir, severely degrading the fleet's mine-sweeping capabilities. They had been tapped for the mission because the stretched HH-53s, specifically designed for special operations, were too long to fit in the elevators of most aircraft carriers without time-consuming rotor blade removal, a problem that persists today.

Members of all armed services generally agreed with the Holloway Report's findings, and some organizational, equipment, and training improvements were made. Under pressure from Congress, the Department of Defense attempted, unsuccessfully, to put an end to interservice rivalries by advocating

A Pave Low Jockey wearing AN/PVS-5A night-vision goggles. Even relatively lightweight goggles require that a counterweight be attached to the back of a pilot's helmet, and after a year of night flying an airman's collar size often increases a size or two from the increased exercise of the neck muscles.

that the Army become the sole operator of rotary-wing special operations assets, while the Air Force continued to develop its long-range fixed-wing capability. Although this particular proposal went nowhere fast because of both congressional backpedaling and continued resistance within the Air Force to anything that would cut into its turf, the future security of the nation was immeasurably enhanced by passage of the 1987 Defense Authorization Act, which established a unified command incorporating the Special Operations Forces from all services. The new Special Operations Command (SOCOM) could train and deploy forces throughout the world and was given the authority to develop and acquire equipment, services, and supplies peculiar to special operations. Of particular interest to DELTA was funding and authorization to modify existing aircraft and develop new helicopter variants.

Under the act, the UH-60 Black Hawk would be reconfigured into three basic models to support all services. The Army's 160th Special Operations Aviation Regiment (Airborne), SOAR(A), would use the MH-60K Pave Hawk to replace its less-capable MH-60As* in the assault role; the HH-60H Rescue Hawk would enhance the Navy's search-and-rescue and special warfare capability; and the Air Force MH-60G Pave Hawk would both replace aging search-and-rescue aircraft and act as an armed escort for the new MH-53J Pave Low IIIs just entering service. All aircraft would be provided with tiedowns to allow shipboard operations.

The L variant Black Hawks, with their more-powerful engines, upgraded transmissions, and hover infrared suppression subsystem (HIRSS) did not enter service until 1988. All MH-60As and many UH-60As have since been retrofitted with the HIRSS.

The newest Pave Low III variant of the CH-53, called the MH-53J, was tasked to perform the heavy-lift rotary-wing effort for the near future. A superb special operations aircraft, it is, unfortunately, rather short-legged, and even with the addition of a 600-gallon fuel bladder, it requires frequent air refueling during long missions. Congressional sponsors of the 1987 legislation—as well as the Air Force hierarchy—envisioned that it

would be phased out of special operations and into search and rescue as MH-47Es came on line.

The special operations variant of the venerable heavy-lift CH-47D Chinook would complement the MH-60K's mission. Unlike the Pave Low IIIs, MH-47Es can easily fit into the elevators of all aircraft carriers and, thus, offers planners more deployment options. The MH-47E also has an avionics system interoperable with its smaller cousin and can engage in full and open competition with the CV-22A Osprey for long-range strategic special operations missions. Unfortunately, the extremely versatile tilt-rotor Osprey, which incorporated the lift, range, and speed of a fixed-wing transport with the vertical-lift capability of a helicopter, remains plagued by mechanical difficulties.

Unlike other special operations helicopters, the AH-6 and MH-6 Little Birds were not dealt with in the published versions of congressional defense appropriations until recently. These descendants of the trusty old Cayuse were developed and fielded through the use of covert funds in much the same way as the F-117 stealth attack aircraft and, interestingly, started to edge out of the black at approximately the same time as the F-117, primarily because of their high visibility during the 1987–1988 retaliatory attacks on Iranian targets in the Persian Gulf and the 1989 overthrow of Panamanian dictator Manuel Noriega.

The 160th SOAR aviators, which carry out these operations, are known as the night stalkers because of their effective use of darkness during missions, and many of these pilots have logged 2,000 or more flight hours wearing night-vision goggles. The regiment, headquartered at Fort Campbell, Kentucky, is composed of four battalions: the 1st with 18 AH-6s, 18 MH-6s, and 30 MH-60s (incorporating the forward-deployed 617th Special Operations Aviation Detachment [Airborne] in Panama); the 2nd with 24 MH-47s; the 3rd with 10 MH-60s and eight MH-47s, based at Hunter Army Airfield, Savannah, Georgia, to support the 1st Ranger Battalion as it did during the Grenada operation; and an Oklahoma National Guard battalion, the 1/245, based at Tulsa, Oklahoma, with more than three dozen aircraft, including 15 UH-60Ls, which will eventually be replaced by MH-60s.

out their orders and apprehend the hijackers, a tense situation developed between the senior U.S. officer present and Italian officers. The situation quickly degenerated, and the *carabonari* drew their trusty Berettas on the equally well-armed SEALs until diplomats intervened, explaining that it was in everyone's best interest to let the Italians take charge.

Yet another incident occurred the following month, when a commercial airliner was hijacked to Malta by Palestinian extremists. This time, DELTA was on hand but not used. In fact,

DELTA was initially not even allowed to land. Since the hijacked aircraft was Egyptian, that country's commandos, trained by U.S. special operations personnel, were allowed to conduct the takedown. Things turned sour, and 57 hostages lost their lives.

Troubles at Home

From 1970 through the mid-1980s, more than 1,000 Americans were killed, taken hostage, or otherwise injured by foreign terrorists. Virtually all of these incidents occurred overseas, but

Throughout the 1970s and 1980s, terrorists in Germany were like fish in a sea of nationalist extremists and sympathizers. (A) A masked demonstrator protests outside the U.S. air base at Rhein-Main, and (B) an arms cache believed to have been hidden by Germany's Red Army Faction. Terrorist groups rely heavily on hidden caches of arms and other supplies.

The unmarked limousine of General Frederick Krossen, commander of U.S. Army forces in Europe, after a failed assassination attempt by Germany's Red Army Faction in September 1981. Only a month earlier, the general had finally heeded the advice of West German counterterrorists and obtained the special armored Mercedes that deflected the blast of a Soviet-made rocket-propelled grenade (RPG) away from the car's interior. In the car was the general, his wife, an aid, and a German driver/bodyguard.

CT planners believed that a terrorist attack could occur on American soil. The 1984 Los Angeles Summer Olympics was an awfully tempting target. As part of the $1 billion effort to provide security against possible attacks, DELTA deployed to a nearby naval facility and stood ready to counter any terrorist situation. Along with DELTA was a massive CT force incorporating city and state SWAT (special weapons and tactics) teams and the FBI's hostage rescue team (HRT).

Not all monies funneled through Army covert accounts were spent wisely or even legitimately. Army auditors discovered a number of irregularities in a covert account between 1981 and 1983. A disturbing amount of double-dipping had taken place, with a hot-air balloon and a Rolls-Royce purchased to supposedly support clandestine operations.

In a climate that one DELTA member described as sheer hysteria, standard cost-accounting techniques were applied to ongoing covert operations and training. The result was dozens of reprimands and perhaps a score or more transfers as nonjudicial punishments in lieu of court-martials. But some soldiers, deservingly, weren't so lucky. In one case, an ISA lieutenant colonel who supported DELTA created a firm as a conduit for covert funds and misappropriated more than $50,000 in just six months. In a series of discreet court-martials and a civil criminal trial running through 1986, at least two officers were sentenced to prison.

For most DELTA troopers, though, life continued its grueling hurry-up-and-wait pace. Troopers provided advice and support to CT units around the world, and a team was quickly dispatched to Willemstad, Curacao, in the Dutch Antilles, to assist in the takedown of a hijacked Venezuelan DC-9. Both fanatics were killed and 79 passengers were freed. Meanwhile, in Lebanon, kidnappings continued unabated and two hostages were murdered: CIA station chief William Buckley in 1985 and Marine Colonel William Higgins in 1989. Frequent movement of hostages and the lack of solid U.S. intelligence sources within the terrorists' camp prevented rescues attempts, and at least one major DELTA /SEAL operation was scrubbed.

Sometimes a scrubbed mission was good news, such as when the vulnerable Statue of Liberty centennial celebration passed without incident in July 1986. On other occasions, events took care of themselves—as in San Salvador and Manila. On

MH-6 Little Birds of the 160th SOAR operating in the Persian Gulf. Among other operations, they took part in the September 1987 capture of an Iranian mine-laying vessel that threatened oil tanker traffic.

A West German wanted poster for known terrorists. As various fugitives were apprehended or killed, they were crossed off the poster by the U.S. counterterrorist team that mounted it on their headquarters' wall.

West Berlin police sift through the rubble of the La Belle discotheque, a bar popular with American servicemen, where a soldier and several Turkish women were killed by a bomb. Intelligence analysts soon discovered that the explosives were planted by Libyan agents based at their embassy in communist East Berlin.

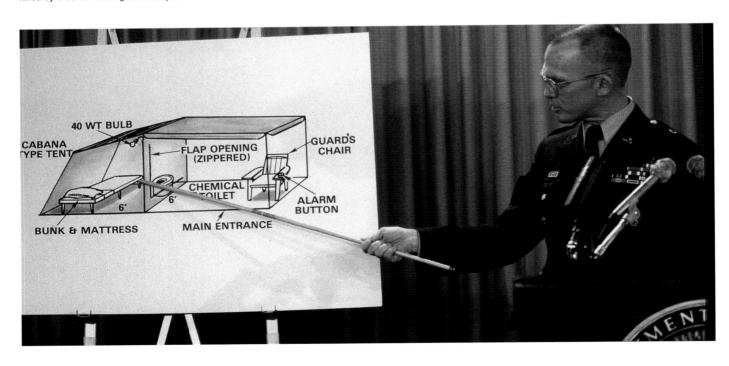

General Dozier's kidnappers erected a tent inside a safe house room to hold their prisoner. Dozier displays a diagram of the tent and nearest guard position after Italian counterterrorists forcibly freed him from the Red Brigade.

November 21, 1989, DELTA was dispatched to the Salvadoran capital of San Salvador to rescue Green Beret trainers trapped in the Sheraton Hotel during a guerrilla offensive. The trainers escaped unharmed, however, before the detachment could be put into action. Almost two weeks later, DELTA received another alert for a possible rescue attempt, this time in the Philippines. American citizens were trapped by an army coup d'etat, but emerged unscathed when the revolt fizzled.

Berlin presented a more interesting—and long-lasting—problem for U.S., as well as British and French, CT units stationed in the city's Western sectors. Along the seven crossing points through the Berlin Wall, Communist East German border guards, called *Vopos*, checked passports to prevent East Germans from passing into the West, while British, French, and American guards allowed people to pass unimpeded both ways, since they didn't, for political reasons, view East Berlin as a foreign territory. So potential terrorists could simply cross into the West from East Berlin, where the Syrians, Libyans, Iranians, and even the PLO, maintained diplomatic missions. A U.S. hasty-response team was always on a high state of alert, and an active exchange program was conducted with DELTA. They operated in close conjunction with Berlin's other Western security organizations, but could not prevent terrorist attacks like the April 5, 1986, bombing of the La Belle discotheque, a club frequented by many American

(A) The U.S. Army's hasty response team in Berlin and several DELTA troopers pose for a group photo during a break in a training exercise. (B) During antiterrorist training in West Berlin, an American serviceman is snatched by a group of mock terrorists.

MH-47E Chinook and MH-60 Black Hawk Variants

The MH-47E's highly advanced integrated avionics system and extended range allow it to complete clandestine deep-penetration missions. The aircraft can easily use map-of-the-earth tactics at night and perform in any weather conditions while placing a minimum workload on the pilot. Special operations enhanced UH-60 Black Hawks have performed spectacularly in long-range combat operations from Grenada to Iraq. All of these helicopters wear infrared-suppressing paint.

MH-60G Pave Hawks conduct an in-flight refueling operation.

Beginning in the early 1990s, MH-60 Pave Hawks have performed spectacularly in long-range combat operations from Grenada to Iraq. All of these helicopters wear infrared-suppressing paint.

servicemen, in which two people were killed and 230 were injured. The twilight world of terrorism and counterterrorism, espionage and counterespionage, did not end until the East German communist system finally collapsed of its own weight, bringing the Berlin Wall down with it.

Throughout all the frustrations and false starts, DELTA troopers maintained their high degree of professionalism and managed to keep their sometimes-irreverent sense of humor. All knew that the beeper clipped to their belts could beep at any time to signal a recall and they'd casually drop whatever they were doing with an offhand, "Looks like it's time to head on back to the Ranch,"* and disappear out the door.

Operation *Just Cause*

A public affairs release from Operation *Just Cause* stated simply that all units from the special operations command participated. DELTA's most publicized mission was the rescue of an American businessman and rotary club member held in

continued on page 79

(A) The MH-6J Little Bird that lifted Kirt Muse to freedom is moved out of the street by U.S. mechanized forces after they secured the area around General Manuel Noriega's headquarters. Note the three-man troop seats along each side and the large crane-like appendage for fast-rope operations. It folds forward against the side of the bird when not in use and inadvertently prevents an easy exit from the interior's right side. (B) The battered *Comandancia*, located just across the street from Muse's prison cell. *Soldier of Fortune*

MH-53 Pave Low III

The MH-53H and MH-53J Pave Low IIIs are descended from a long line of Sikorsky helicopters that have performed rescue and special operations from the Korean War through Vietnam and through the aborted 1980 raid to free American hostages in Iran. Of a family that is second only to the Soviet-built Mi-26 Halo in size and heavy-lift capability, the Pave Low III is capable of operating with pinpoint accuracy in all weather and light conditions. It also shares many components with other Air Force assets, such as the forward-looking infrared (FLIR) on the AC-130 Specter gunships and MC-130 Combat Talon transports.

B

600gal internal auxiliary fuel bladder

GPS antenna

Two rear AN/ALQ-162 electronic countermeasures (ECM) antennas

Pintle mount for machine gun or minigun (ramp)

Rescue hoist

Two crash-worthy 650gal external auxiliary fuel tanks

Two forward AN/ALQ-162 ECM antennas

Retractable inflight refueling probe

AN/AAQ-10 FLIR imager

Two AN/ALQ-152(V)2 infrared countermeasures jammers on outrigger pylons

Two pintle mounts for machine guns or miniguns (forward side windows

AN/ALR-69(V)6 radar warning reciever

AN/APQ-158(V)2 TF/TA radar

Infrared searchlight

Plus fast-rope rappelling system, flare/chaff dispensers and SATCO

Close-ups of a .50-caliber machine gun (A) and 7.62mm mini-gun (B) on pintle mounts bolted to Pave Low III deck ramps. "Ma deuce"—the reliable .50-caliber—continues to provide outstanding service to the special operations community, and the deadly mini-gun has proven its worth from Vietnam to Iraq.

The MH-53H and MH-53J Pave Low IIIs are descended from a long line of Sikorsky helicopters that have performed rescue and special operations from the Korean War through the aborted 1980 raid to free American hostages in Iran. From a family that is second only to the Soviet-built Mi-26 Halo in size and heavy-lift capability, the Pave Low III is capable of operating with pinpoint accuracy in all weather conditions and at night. It also shares many components with other Air Force assets, such as the forward-looking infrared (FLIR) on the AC-130 Specter gunships. (C) An MH-53J Enhanced Pave Low III is parked between two veteran special operations aircraft, the MH-53H Pave Low and the MH-60G Pave Hawk. (D) A team of special operators is inserted by fast-rope operations into the target area from an MH-53H Pave Low.

Little Bird Variants

Based on an extremely popular airframe that can be found in extensive use by both civilian and government entities in every corner of the globe, the Little Bird offers great agility, adaptability, and its own version of visual stealth if warranted by a mission. The aircraft is manufactured by McDonnell Douglas and carries a basic civilian designation of either MD 500 or MD 530. The 500, 500C, and 500D aircraft were produced with a round bubble-like nose through 1982 when all subsequent helicopters of these types were manufactured with the more pointed nose of the MD 500E, 500F, and 500MG, as well as the slightly larger and more powerful MD 520 and 530 series aircraft. The U.S. Army's orders for these helicopters after 1982, however, have generally called for the retention of the bubble nose to maintain the option of installing a TOW antitank missile aiming sight and to keep visual commonality with the large number of pre-1982, nonmilitary aircraft of this type.

The high civilian and foreign military demand for a small, reliable, inexpensive helicopter was coupled with the manufacturer's effort to fill that demand by incorporating a large variety of powerplant, transmission, rotor, and other changes on what is essentially the same airframe. This proliferation of different aircraft types found its way into the 160th SOAR's inventory since there was never a specific production line opened for the U.S. Army, all purchases being made in bits and pieces over a decade of off-the-shelf buying to supplement the original OH-6A Cayuse helicopters. This proliferation has led to a mind-boggling alphabet soup of aircraft types in the 160th's 1st Battalion, the unit that most directly supports DELTA. Jane's All the World's Aircraft states that the MH-6B and AH-6C are derived from the

An AH-6 Little Bird pokes its nose into some tight areas looking for terrorist targets.

OH-6A; the AH-6F and MH-6E from MD 500MG; and the AH-6G, MH-6F, and MH-6J from the MD 530MG. "A" designations are given to the heavily armed attack versions of the Little Bird, which can be armed with a variety of miniguns, machine guns, rockets, and missiles. Nearly all Little Birds are equipped with a

(left) A "sterile" 160th SOAR AH-60 Little Bird bereft of any identifying marks; (top) an MD-530N equipped with the NOTAR (no tail rotor) system, including close-up of steering louvers on the underside of the tail; (bottom) and an MD-530N configured for transportation with the louver cone and tail fins folded upward and the main rotor blades stowed along the tail boom. Note that the MD-530 models have both the pointed nose for streamlining and the pre-1982 bubble nose of the MD-500-series aircraft.

swinging crane-like arm for fast-rope rappelling and Stabo operations, and the AH-6G, MH-6E, MH-6F, and possibly the AH-6F, have multifunction displays and forward-looking infrared (FLIR) imagers to be used with night-vision goggles.

Of great benefit to DELTA in urban counterterrorist situations is the 160th SOAR's conversion to the NOTAR system on its Little Birds. NOTAR uses a variable-pitch fan and direct jet thruster to push cool air through longitudinal steering louvers on a circulation-control tailboom. Although early tests by the 160th showed higher-than-desired pilot workloads due to a tendency for the nose to wander at low speeds, yaw-only stability augmentation corrected the problem. With the NOTAR system, AH/MH-6 aircraft display a greatly reduced acoustic signature, increased hover stability, and roughly double the lateral and rearward speeds of conventional helicopters. The absence of a tail rotor also eliminates the danger of tail strikes on ground crews and allows DELTA troopers more freedom of movement around the aircraft during operations.

AC-130 Specter Gunship

The AC-130 Specter gunship is a basic C-130 modified with side-mounted weapons and sensors that make it highly adaptable to a variety of special missions. When fielded against targets with few antiaircraft defenses and a minimal air threat, the Specter is able to provide close air support much more efficiently than a large force of fighter aircraft and is a particularly effective platform for interdiction and armed reconnaissance missions. The Specter has the ability to aid in perimeter defense, escort, surveillance, search and rescue, infiltration/exfiltration, illumination, and landing zone support operations, as well as to conduct limited airborne command and control functions for other strike aircraft.

The AC-130H is armed with two 20mm Gatling-type guns, a rapid-firing 40mm cannon and 105mm howitzer supported by a laser rangefinder (which can also be used to mark targets for laser-guided bombs), an infrared sensor to identify heat sources such as people and vehicles, a beacon-tracking radar, a fire-control computer, a two-kilowatt searchlight, and a low-light-level television capable of amplifying even faint traces of starlight to monitor both targets and friendly forces. The newer AC-130U models have retained the 40mm and 105mm weapons but use a single 25mm Gatling-type gun fed by a two-canister automated loading system instead of the H models' 20mm guns, which require their linked ammunition to be hand loaded. Other new features have also been added, including the F-15's fire-control radar, lightweight Kevlar armor, inflight refueling capability, and a highly efficient soundproof battle management center.

Depending on the target, threat environment, weather, and desired level of destruction, weapons can be accurately employed at altitudes from 3,000 to 20,000 feet above ground level. The Specter fires from a constant angle of bank and, at a typical slant range of 10,000 feet, the remarkably stable gun platform can deliver ordnance within 10 feet of its target even under conditions of low cloud ceilings or poor visibility. Unlike fighter aircraft, which must make separate runs on hostile forces, targets are continually visible throughout the gunship's orbit and can be fired on at will. But even though the run-in headings required by fighter aircraft are not needed, no-fire headings may be imposed from the ground or automatically computed by the aircrew if there is a risk of short rounds hitting friendly forces from a particular angle.

An AC-130 Specter lines up a target.

The 105mm gun crew on an AC-130 Specter gunship reloads during a fire mission.

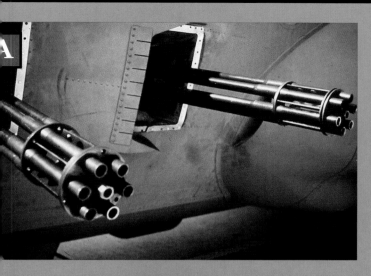

(A) Twin 20mm Gatling-type guns aft of the cockpit and (B) 40mm and 105mm guns forward of the aircraft's loading ramp.

The Specter's two-kilowatt searchlight can be used to illuminate targets and landing zones, aid in search and rescue, and supply light for the television sensor if its illuminator is inoperative. In combat, the searchlight is normally used in a covert infrared mode to provide illumination for night-vision devices, since its overt white light mode would easily pinpoint the gunship's position for hostile forces.

Delta troopers in a tight spot can mark their ground position with a wide variety of items. First, Mk-6 and Mk-25 ground markers can be dropped by hand from the rear of the Specter and will burn for 45 and 30 minutes, respectively. Next, transponders can be picked up by the aircraft's beacon-tracking radar at up to

10 nautical miles, and the powerful AN/UPN-25 and SST-181x transponders can be received by the ship's navigation radar at up to 60 nautical miles. A standard survival vest strobe light with a removable infrared filter can also be used either visually or with the filter installed. The infrared filter provides the same information to the aircrew as the unmasked strobe but prevents visible light from revealing the friendly ground position to the enemy forces. Positive identification is provided by turning one or more strobes off and on in response to radio instructions from the aircrew. The old standby, lightweight 3x5-foot cloth reflective panels can clearly mark ground reference points when illuminated by the Specter, either overtly or covertly.

Panama's notorious Modelo Prison. Kurt Muse was a resident of Panama and, in concert with fellow Panamanian rotarians (dubbed the "rotarians from Hell" by *Soldier of Fortune* magazine), had been causing Panama's strongman, Manuel Noriega, trouble by operating a clandestine radio station, filling the air waves with propaganda and, in some instances, reporting misleading or confusing instructions to the Panamanian Defense Forces (PDF) on military radio frequencies. Muse had been part of a psychological operation (PSYOP) mission against Noriega and was eventually turned in by the wife of a former co-conspirator. He was jailed at Modelo, located a stone's throw from Noriega's command post/headquarters-turned-fortress, the *Comandancia*.

In the early morning hours of December 19, 1989, Muse was rescued by members of Delta in a classic CT operation. Transported to the rooftop of the prison by an MH-6, the

assault team, backed up by a man on the inside who disabled the facility's emergency generator, cleared the upper floors from the top down and fought its way to the holding area where Muse was imprisoned. Armed with MP5s of various configurations, the troopers took out the armed guards with lethal shock and firepower and used just enough explosives to open the door without harming Muse. Two troopers fought their way to Muse's cell, two more provided security on the stairwell, and four more were on the roof, exchanging fire with prison guards in the barracks beyond a small courtyard. The operation, so far, had unfolded with the clockwork precision of a Wally World exercise. As the security and rescue teams loaded into the helo and along its outside-mounted seats, the heavily laden Little Bird lifted into the night sky.

Meanwhile, AC-130s tore great chunks out of the *Comandancia*'s defenses, tracers streamed toward Black Hawk

MC-130 Combat Talon and HC-130 Combat Shadow

The mission of the MC-130E and MC-130H Combat Talons is to conduct day and night infiltration, exfiltration, resupply, psychological operations, and aerial reconnaissance into hostile or enemy-controlled territory using air landings, air drops, or surface-to-air recoveries. Forward-looking infrared (FLIR) imagers enable aircrews to visually identify targets and checkpoints at night, while terrain-following/terrain-avoidance (TF/TA) radar and an inertial navigation system allow extreme accuracy while navigating to unmarked drop zones. Missions are normally flown at night using a high-low high-altitude profile. The high

An MC-130E Combat Talon infiltrates enemy airspace while training for a resupply mission of unconventional forces.

A) During a permission inspection, the pilot and crew chief of an MC-130E examine the Fulton Recovery System with the nose prongs extended and (B) the "yoke" retracted.

portion is flown prior to penetrating and after exiting the target area at an altitude that minimizes fuel consumption and enemy detection. The aircraft then descends to the lowest possible altitude consistent with flying safety and uses its TF/TA radar to penetrate and operate in hostile territory.

The Talon's range depends on several factors, including configuration, payload, en route winds and weather, and the length of time spent at fuel-guzzling low-level flight. For planning purposes, its range (without refueling and factoring in two hours at low level) is 2,800 nautical miles. With inflight refueling, the Talon's range is limited only by the availability of tanker support and the effect that crew fatigue may have on the mission. The Talon is not a rapid-response aircraft. Operating deep in heavily defended enemy territory requires extensive preflight planning, and units normally receive notification at least 48 hours out with a final briefing on threats and positions of friendly forces before takeoff.

Aircrews are capable of successfully operating at unmarked drop zones (DZs) but usually have something they can hang their headphones on. When ground and air component commanders agree to use a specific DZ, reception committee personnel coordinate with the aircrew on the type of markings to be used, configuration of the DZ, method of authentication, and release point determination. The most frequent cause for mission aborts is a lack of coordination or confusion over marking procedures: It is important to note that terrain following is made difficult during moderate showers and is even further degraded during heavy thunderstorms.

Depending on the mission, an aircrew makes either a static-line, low-altitude air drop; a high-altitude, low-opening (HALO) air drop; a surface-to-air recovery (STAR) using a Fulton extraction system; or simply lands the aircraft. For static-line drops during

mately 120 miles per hour, the Shadow's customer slowly edges its refuel probe closer to the drogue-tipped hose while making certain that it stays beneath or to the outside of the tanker's turbulent slipstream. It generally takes an MH-53 less than 10 minutes to top off and an MH-47, with its huge fuel blisters, can get its fill in about 15 minutes.

(A) MC-130E crewmen check the console of electronic countermeasures during an infiltration exercise. (B) MH-53J Pave Low helicopters swing into position to begin in-flight refueling operations.

combat operations, a Talon is flown as low as 750 feet, while a HALO drop, which requires a free fall before parachute opening, is never conducted from lower than 1,500 feet. For static-line drops combining both men and equipment (such as rubber rafts), troops exit immediately after ejection of equipment. A STAR can be used for extractions during day or night but requires fairly good weather to accomplish the mission safely. Either two people or 500 pounds of equipment can be picked up over land or water per pass. During air landings, the minimum length necessary is the takeoff/landing roll plus 500 feet for a total of approximately 3,000 feet. The Talon's minimum required runway width is 60 feet and, while the capability exists to set down at a landing zone that has no lights or is lit with infrared lights, use of the special forces seven-light panel marking system (which includes a 250-foot/10 percent safety zone at each end out) is preferred.

The HC-130P Combat Shadow tankers have essentially the same extensive radar and navigational aids as the Combat Talon, as well as the ability to refuel two helicopters simultaneously in flight. After the tanker unreels its fuel line and slows to approxi-

helicopters, and conventional mechanized infantry forces brought maximum pressure to bear on the PDF in the streets below. The overloaded chopper was hit by ground fire and landed with an unceremonial thud on the street below. The iron-nerved aviator maneuvered it down the street like a taxi and pulled into a parking lot. Using several tall apartment buildings as a shield, the pilot again tried to make his getaway, but the Little Bird was knocked down again, this time for good, and the men formed a defensive perimeter nearby. Seconds after one DELTA trooper held up an infrared strobe light, they were spotted by a Black Hawk, and three 6th Infantry Regiment M-113 armored personnel carriers came to the rescue. Four DELTA troopers were hurt, one seriously, but unlike the events some nine years earlier in Iran, this plan was executed successfully.

Chapter 5

BACK TO THE DESERT

A thirsty trooper inhales bottled water in the shade of a C-141 StarLifter in Saudi Arabia.

The deep sleep of the early morning hours was interrupted by the familiar sound of a pager. Reaching for his clothing, the young sergeant kissed his wife and went to check on his son. The trooper bent down to kiss the boy goodbye as he had so often in the past. He then pulled on his well-worn cowboy boots, climbed into his pickup truck, and drove to the post. In less than two hours, the young sergeant's troop was winging away from Pope Air Force Base near Fort Bragg. As the wheels of the lumbering C-141 StarLifter retracted into their wells, his troop commander was already scanning the initial intelligence reports from the agencies supporting the unit. Things were not so good in the land of oil and sand.

On the morning of August 2, 1990, mechanized elements of Saddam Hussein's elite republican guards stabbed across the desert frontier separating Iraq and Kuwait east of the disputed Rumalia oil field. Iraqi forces had been massing steadily across the border for almost two weeks before the invasion, but both Western and Arabian governments believed this to be nothing more than a show of force to bolster Hussein's financial claims against the oil-rich kingdom. By midday, all meaningful resistance by Kuwait's tiny army had been crushed, and its royal family had fled to a sumptuous exile in Saudi Arabia.

The Baathist government in Baghdad rejoiced over its seemingly quick victory and believed that it had been accomplished with such speed that the world was presented with a *fait accompli*. Hussein expected a toothless condemnation from the United Nations and perhaps even a half-hearted economic embargo that would soon fade away. U.S. and British leaders meeting in the United States immediately resolved that the rest of the Middle East's oil resources must be kept out of Hussein's bloodied hands, at all costs. Even before Hussein's generals gathered their forces for the next morning's move to the Saudi border, numerous elements of America's Special Operations Forces were either deployed or going "wheels up" from bases in the United States and Europe.

From the moment President George H. W. Bush was notified that Iraqi forces were forging across Kuwait's border, one of the prime challenges he faced was the possibility—indeed probability—that many Americans would become prisoners in a dangerous diplomatic game. The specter of another major Middle East hostage crisis loomed over the Pentagon and the White House. And no one needed to be reminded that the Carter administration fell because of the prolonged hostage crisis in Iran. Plus, the U.S. Embassy staff and numerous Americans associated with Kuwait's petroleum industry were extremely vulnerable. When coupled with the Baathist regime's close ties with terrorist groups, history of wanton aggression against its neighbors, and deadly abuse of its own people, the president had no choice but to act. Although Special Operations Forces assets already in the Gulf were capable of performing a hasty-option response, the National Command Authority launched the first DELTA assets into the Middle East. Initially, DELTA assets were deployed as bodyguards, but senior commanders soon recognized that DELTA assets could be better used on other, more critical missions.

Crisis action teams were dispatched to Saudi Arabia and other friendly nations to establish C^3 (command, control, and communications) sites for future operations and to provide a terminal for information to and from Washington. Launch sites for missions were identified and staging areas hastily opened. Meanwhile, back at Fort Bragg, the Joint Special Operations Command (JSOC) began building a massive workup of target folders for the long war that was sure to come.

An Iraqi television picture of Saddam Hussein and a "guest."

All-terrain fast attack vehicles (FAVs) and motorcycles saw extensive use by Special Operations Forces, including DELTA, in Iraq and Kuwait and operated from forward bases in Saudi Arabia or base camps established far behind Iraqi lines. Motorcycles with heavily muffled engines offered troopers individualized, high-speed movement, coupled with the ability to approach a target from several axes simultaneously and, on some types of missions, were used in combination with FAVs.
Soldier of Fortune

A C-130 of unidentified type sits baking under "big red" across from a special operations Black Hawk with external add-on fuel tanks. DELTA operated out of secure, remote bases dotting the desert wastes south of the Saudi-Iraqi border.

All-terrain fast attack vehicles (FAVs).

Elements of the Intelligence Support Activity (ISA) were also moving into the area. Like so many parts of the special operations force, ISA was an offshoot of the *Desert I* after-action review. The lack of information from human intelligence (HUMINT) sources was a critical failing during the hostage crisis in Iran. DELTA did not have an eyeball on its target in Iran. In Iraq and Kuwait, ISA would provide the needed eyes.

Various elements of the myriad special operations units in Europe and the United States continued to move in, and most of the burden of working with the resistance inside Kuwait was assumed by special forces units in accordance with theater war plans. As predicted, U.S. and other foreign nationals did indeed become "guests" at selected Iraqi strategic military and nuclear sites but were eventually allowed to leave as a "gesture of good will" when their continued captivity threatened to precipitate, not prevent, an assault on Iraq. DELTA remained.

Commencement of the coalition air campaign raised fears that hostages might be taken around the globe, and additional

target folders of possible hostage-holding centers were created. While significant terrorist operations never emerged, the public display of Allied prisoners of war did cause concern at the highest levels, and plans were formulated to rescue those individuals. Small teams were also selected to carry out a number of sensitive direct-action missions against targets in Iraq's command-and-control nets.

Special Operations Forces had to determine how to get the conventional force commanders to use their capabilities properly or even at all. For example, the 75th Ranger Regiment's assessment team left the Gulf after discovering that there was very little they could do in the theater, and the 82nd Airborne Division was severely handicapped on the billiard table–like terrain without an immense amount of support.

(A) A Scud B medium-range ballistic missile on its MAZ-543 transporter-erector-launcher (TEL) and (B) a rare photograph of a Scud impact. Even before changes were made to the weapon that degraded its accuracy, the Scud was not known for its ability to make pinpoint strikes. This weapon was fired by Soviet forces at Afghan guerrillas who had surrounded Loyalist troops at an isolated garrison. It missed the guerrillas and landed instead within the government troops' defensive perimeter.

Soldier of Fortune

Scud-hunting Delta troopers check their gear in a wadi during their long-range patrol deep in Iraq. The urgent mission forced General Schwarzkopf to draw on his only uncommitted special operators: Delta and the SAS. Note the ad hoc camouflage of hurriedly spray-painted squiggles on the vehicles.

Colonel Jesse Johnson, commander of Central Command's (CENTCOM's) Special Operations Command (SOC), drafted his campaign plans for the upcoming desert war from his headquarters at King Fahd International Airport near Dhahran. A veteran of *Desert I*, where he commanded the joint Ranger- DELTA road-watch teams, Johnson knew what difficulties awaited his forces. Luckily, his boss at CENTCOM, General H. Norman Schwarzkopf, had the utmost confidence in his special ops commander. Despite attempts by elements within the joint chiefs of staff to replace him with a two-star officer, Schwarzkopf kept his faith in Johnson, who in return became the architect for several brilliantly executed operations.

Hussein's Vengeance Weapon

As the war progressed, the Scud B medium-range ballistic missile, successor to Hitler's infamous V-1 and V-2 rockets of World War II, was unleashed. The Scud retained many of the V-2's basic characteristics, along with many deadly improvements. Highly mobile, it nevertheless required more than an hour to fuel and its involved targeting procedures took excruciatingly long to complete, even when performed by experienced crews at preplotted sites. Plus, homemade versions of the missile, like the *al Hussein*, incorporated range enhancements that both reduced its warhead capacity and severely degraded its ability to strike near its target.

Troopers viewed through an NVG rappel from a Black Hawk.

A night-stalking F-15 takes on fuel during *Desert Storm*.

The Soviets designed the Scud to deliver small nuclear warheads or to function as an area saturation system when fired in conventional battery salvos; the Iraqis instead used it as a fire-in-the-general-direction-of-your-adversary-and-then-wait-for-the-results weapon, intended principally to terrorize their neighbors. Fixed launch sites containing both real and dummy missiles existed at airfields in western Iraq, targeting Israel, and in eastern Iraq, aimed at Iran and Saudi Arabia. These sites were well known to U.S. and Israeli planners and could be easily destroyed. It was Hussein's surprisingly large number of wheeled Scud and Frog missile launchers that proved to be exceedingly difficult targets for air reconnaissance assets to locate. That set the stage for one role DELTA troopers never dreamed of or trained for: Scud hunting.

Many, if not all, of the troops deployed to the Gulf had extensive training in their initial special forces specialties and were already experts in carrying out such standard missions as unconventional warfare, special reconnaissance, foreign internal defense, and search-and-rescue operations, to name a few. But it was the introduction of Hussein's terror weapons that forced the counterterrorists to revert to these basic war-fighting specialties and become what the press dubbed "super commandos." The war was going poorly for Hussein, and he knew that his best bet was to drive a wedge between the Arab and Western elements in the coalition arrayed against him. If attacks on Jewish population centers could push Israel into a knee-jerk military response, Hussein believed that indignant Arab masses would finally heed his call for a jihad, or holy war, and either overthrow unfriendly governments like President Hosni Mubarak's in Egypt or, at the very least, force their governments to withdraw from the coalition. Western elements would be isolated and forced into an ignominious withdrawal.

Hussein's strategy wasn't difficult to anticipate, and the White House made strong public statements (coupled with a rapid, showy deployment of a Patriot surface-to-air missile battery to Tel Aviv) that drawing Israel into the war would be prevented at all costs. CENTCOM had no choice but to commit its Air Force component to a resource-consuming search for mobile launchers with little to show for its efforts.* This same mission was also handed to the Army's special forces, which, if necessary, would target individual vehicles for air strikes—an extremely risky business for the troops involved but a very important mission in light of the strategic situation. But CENTCOM quickly discovered that there was a critical shortage of trained special recon teams in the Kuwaiti Theater of Operations (KTO).

Special operations assets, primarily DELTA and the desert-wise SAS, were formed into teams and prepared for the upcoming operations. At first, though, Colonel Johnson's professionals from Smoke Bomb Hill and the Ranch were understandably missing from the almost-continuous Gulf news coverage, while other forces from Fort Bragg, the XVIIIth Airborne Corps, the 1st Corps Support Command, and the 82nd Airborne Division, received their share of the limelight.

Prepping the Battlefield

An in-depth mission analysis was conducted on the upcoming Scud hunt by the intelli-

A special operator has time to reflect as he is flown to a high-altitude, low-opening (HALO) insertion. Note the altimeter on the soldier's left wrist.

gence agencies supporting the theater's Special Operations Forces. Intel experts scrutinized the terrain and infiltration/exfiltration routes through Iraqi antiaircraft belts, and known locations of enemy units were plotted on situation maps. As this information was analyzed, a clear picture emerged indicating that most target areas could be easily reached by Army MH-60 Pave Hawks of the 160th SOAR or Air Force MH-53 Pave Low IIIs of the 1st Special Operations Wing.

Unfortunately, the extremely heavy demand for specialized helicopters in the KTO, as well as other considerations, meant that they couldn't be used in every situation. For tactical reasons, the target area required a HAHO infiltration. HAHO (pronounced hey-ho), or high-altitude, high-opening, means that a drop is conducted at about 30,000 feet or higher, with the jumper opening his parachute just after clearing the plane. The trooper then glides his maneuverable double-canopy parachute through the sky and lands with pinpoint accuracy at a predetermined site. The distance between ripcord pull and landing point can be as much as 50 miles.

The team is required to prepare a briefback on how each trooper will carry out his duties; this is standard operating

Two HALO experts prepare to land on the drop zone.

An Air Force special operations combat control team member exits from the open ramp of a MC-130 Combat Talon. Control teams are often inserted before the arrival of special operations or conventional forces to mark landing or drop zones that must be used at night by pilots using NVGs and aircraft fitted with infrared imagers. For example, a control team member had already arrived at and marked the *Desert I* refuel site in Iran before the arrival of the aircraft bearing DELTA. The lack of weapon and rucksack indicates that this was taken during a practice exercise.

procedure within the special operations community and covers the friendly-versus-the-enemy situation, the mission, its execution, support requirements, command structures, and a concise, detailed narrative of how the trooper will help accomplish the mission. The briefback, then given to the unit's leaders, not only demonstrates that the men are ready, but also assures the team

A special forces trooper takes up the frog position during a practice jump.

that everyone is playing off the same sheet of music.

After a few questions, the team is given the go-ahead and conducts final rehearsals, equipment checks, and other preparations. On this mission, they're more concerned with the sneak-and-peek than with the direct-action aspects of the operation. If they can find the elusive transporter-erector-launchers (TELs), they'll call in an air strike and, if necessary, use a portable laser to target the weapon for destruction by the Air Force.

The basic plan is simple. The team will move undetected from their drop zone to a hidden observation point overlooking a likely area for Scud activity. When confirmed targets enter the area, SOC will be notified, and an E-2C Sentry's airborne warning and control system (AWACS) will vector strike aircraft into the target area. During their approach, the jets follow voice or signal beacon wavelengths to their prey. Air attacks will be conducted visually, but any TELs obscured by darkness, camouflage, or poor weather will be lased, or painted, by the recon

team. Rolling in on their bomb runs, the fast-movers' sensors will lock on a laser-guided bomb or rocket and release the smart munitions to glide along the laser's invisible path like a road map to the target. The jets will then maneuver away from the area, having only teased the outer perimeters of the lethal antiaircraft systems' kill zones, and DELTA troopers will continue to lase targets as needed. As many Iraqi units discovered, the laser's invisible beam brought very visible destruction.

Reaching the departure airfield, the team is ushered into a secured hangar where the specialized gear for the mission is stored. The departure airfield will also be the mission support site (MSS), and a mobile communications van, mated to the main SOC communications bunker at King Khalid Military City,[*] has been moved into the hangar. The van constitutes part of a duplex communications network that ensures reception of the team's vital intelligence even if one part of the network goes down from either systems failure or enemy action. Meanwhile,

[*]Designed and constructed by the U.S. Army Corps of Engineers during the Iran–Iraq War, King Khalid Military City is one of three huge base complexes around which the outer defenses of the kingdom are formed. The Emerald City (as it was called by many U.S. soldiers, who were surprised at the sight of it rising out of the desert wastes) is located roughly 110 miles southwest of Kuwait's westernmost point, almost halfway to the major Saudi Arabian city of Buraydah.

Above: The control and reporting center outside King Khalid Military City which linked U.S. and Saudi mobile and airborne communications. **Left:** An internal view.

the troopers stay focused on checking and rechecking their weapons and field gear. All weapons are test-fired before leaving the isolation site, and at the hangar a ritual that weds the jumper to his air items and other essential equipment takes place. This union ends only when the mission is completed—or they are parted by death.

The six troopers wear sterile desert camouflage fatigues with the required face scarves and flop hats. Struggling mightily, they pull on cumbersome, insulated jumpsuits to help fight off the cold, which sometimes exceeds –50 degrees Fahrenheit at 35,000 feet, even in the Middle East. In addition to its insulation, the jumpsuits have radar-absorbing capabilities that will impede the enemy's ability to detect the soldiers as they glide across the sky. The February night engulfs the airfield and provides some relief as the men don their parachutes and oxygen masks. Before high-altitude drops like this, both the jumpers and the crew of the unpressurized aircraft

have to start breathing oxygen one hour before takeoff. The team receives final jumpmaster inspections, and the troop commander arrives for one last visit. He is more of a fellow member than a commander, and everyone in the hangar knows how the boss feels. He'd trade in his major's oak leaves to be going with them into Iraq.

Following the safety NCO out into the desert darkness, each man finds his own release to the inevitable tension. Their transportation, a huge C-141B, rests majestically next to the hangar, its gaping clamshell doors exposing the broad tail. The team struggles up the StarLifter's ramp into the cavernous cargo bay, while the crew chief and loadmaster guide the men around the small patches of hydraulic fluid dotting its deck. An oxygen console rests securely in the center of the compartment, and each jumper plugs into it after disconnecting the oxygen mask from his individual bailout bottle.

As the StarLifter slowly pivots and then begins to taxi, the crew chief switches the internal lighting to the red lights required for the team to gain their night vision. The pilot reaches the main runway, and as he revs up the four powerful Pratt & Whitney turbofans for takeoff, each team member is caught in the thoughts of the moment: the myriad details that must be covered so the mission succeeds, his wife, family, or the girl back home—the same thoughts soldiers have had to deal with since the second-oldest profession began.

The Jump

The C-141B flies on an easterly heading to its rendezvous point with two B-52s flying in from the tiny island base of Diego Garcia deep in the Indian Ocean. Snuggling into the number three slot, the formation portrays just another inbound bomber formation for any Iraqi radar still operating.

As the unlikely trio nears Iraqi airspace, the jumpmaster receives updates from the navigator. At prescribed checkpoints, he notifies the team of their exact coordinates so they all know their location in case they're forced to bail out early. Thirty minutes from jump time, the team prepares for the infil. The men make sure their rucksacks ride snugly against the bottom of the main parachute. Checking their padded-leather jump helmets, goggles, and oxygen masks one last time, they prepare to change over from the oxygen consoles to the bailout bottles strapped to their left sides. On command from the jumpmaster, the jumpers switch to their bailout bottles and waddle toward the open troop doors on each side of the fuselage.

Staff Sergeant Len Rodgers and the rest of the recon team work their way to positions along the walls of the StarLifter as their communications man, serving as jumpmaster, completes his visual checks and gives the hand signal for standby. The cabin's eerie red lights, green jump light, and the howling winds whipping in the open troop doors could easily meet the needs of a good nightmare, and Staff Sergeant Rodgers is nearly deafened by the roaring wind and mournful banshee whine of the engines. He marvels that some people actually think this is fun. Moving closer to the door, he receives the "Go!" signal, as the jumpmaster disappears out the open troop door.

Pivoting on the ball of his right foot, Rodgers swings out behind him and falls into the "frog" position. The rest of the team immediately follows in quick succession. Plummeting through the moonless night, arms and legs extended, Rodgers feels the penetrating cold. Behind him, each man monitors the altimeter securely strapped to his left wrist and assumes the glide position as he prepares to deploy his parachute. At 30,000 feet, they pull their silver ripcords.

To the casual observer, this particular maneuver looks like a giant hand shaking each jumper loose from his very life. In reality, the men feel very little, and each checks the double-layer canopy above to see if his is fully inflated. Fortunately for this team, all now resemble airfoil-shaped wings, and the jumpers line up in a rough, follow-the-leader formation, taking the planned westerly heading as Staff Sergeant Rodgers navigates through the frozen night air. Settling into the parachute harness, he scans the panorama unfolding before him. Far to the north, flashes appear from the bombing mission that the team's C-141 had joined. Craning his neck around to the southeast, he can barely make out green[*] tracers darting skyward in a futile search for the destroyers of a known Scud site's command-and-control bunker and wonders if it was done in by one of the F-117 stealth attack aircraft. He turns back and looks toward the unseen drop zone and toys with the idea that the display is for their benefit. He knows, however, that the distant explosions mean that real, flesh-and-blood men are dying.

As the team continues its noiseless flight, each jumper lines up on the dull luminescent strip on the helmet below. Altimeter checks show that the gradual warming they feel is due to the descent. At 12,000 feet, they remove their masks and inhale the night air. With each passing minute, the team gets closer to the drop zone, and this is when they're most vulnerable. They're sure that the entire Iraqi army is waiting to pounce on them, but the only living things awaiting them are some stray goats from a Bedouin camp that run bleating into the night when they strike the earth. The men are relieved that no reception committee is on hand to greet them, but there will be plenty of time for surprises. One of the greatest shocks of this desert war was the fact that whenever you thought you were in the middle of nowhere, someone always showed up—usually at the most inopportune time.

---

[*]Munitions manufactured by former Warsaw Pact countries such as the Soviet Union and Czechoslovakia give off green tracers, but the spectrum of hues sometimes runs to a yellow–green. U.S. and many Western munitions give off a red trace.

Chapter 6

THE SCUD BUSTERS

The Lord said to Moses, "Send men to spy out the land of Canaan. . .
from each tribe of their fathers shall you send a man, everyone a leader among them."
—Numbers 13

Troopers in the desert viewed through an image-intensification device.

The team quickly assembles after landing and moves to a nearby depression; half take up defensive positions, the others strip off their heavy jumpsuits and then roll them up with their 'chutes and jump helmets to make compact bundles. The gear is quickly buried, and the troops silently take their turn guarding the perimeter. Preparing to move out, each man goes through his mental checklist to ensure that every piece of equipment is in place. Faint vehicle noise drifts through the black night, and the telltale signs of light are visible to the south.

Staff Sergeant Christopher Gleason, the point man for this operation, silently moves to his right, where the team leader is making last-minute compass checks and using his handheld satellite navigation system to pinpoint the team's exact location. Chief Warrant Officer Gary Van Hee intently studies the tiny screen of his global positioning system (GPS) unit as Gleason points out the rather obvious activity to the southwest.

Each man's personal equipment is designed for specific tasks. Black balaclavas have been replaced with desert flop hats and face paint of pale yellow and brown. No-sweat bandanas and camouflage scarves are wrapped tightly around necks and tucked into chocolate chip-patterned camouflage jackets. The men carry ammunition in pouches hung from their vests, and distributed about their bodies are canteens, first-aid equipment, a powerful miniature flashlight, and a Beretta pistol. Two men also carry silencers to noiselessly kill enemy guards or inquisitive point men.

The threat of Iraqi poison gas is real, so each trooper carries a gas mask and a protective suit. Rucks are configured with

A special operator programs his global positioning system (GPS) during a lull in the fighting for Baghdad.

The business end of a satellite communications system (SATCOM) during operations near Narizah, Afghanistan.

extra ammunition and smoke grenades. Additional water, medical supplies, food, and limited decontamination gear, complete the major equipment. For weapons, this team carries either Colt M16A2 assault rifles or Heckler & Koch MP5 submachine guns.

Communications expert Sergeant First Class Michael Cranson sends the team's initial entry report, a code-word transmission advising the MSS that they've arrived safely at the drop zone. Cranson uses his radio's burst-transmission capability; the split-second broadcast prevents hostile direction-finders from getting a fix on their position.

Armed with a silenced MP5 SD3, Staff Sergeant Gleason slowly leads the way toward a large, rocky outcropping, as the men fall in behind him in loose file. Gleason and his fellow troopers use AN/PVS-7 night-vision goggles to traverse the rocky terrain. Popularly known as NODs, for night-observation devices, the 1.5-pound goggles fit against a trooper's forehead and illuminate the darkness with an eerie

U.S. Special Operations Forces do not truly "own the night" as the often-repeated slogan claims, but they do operate effectively in that environment, due to a combination of superb training and equipment. Troopers viewed through an NVG move out under cover of darkness.

(A) A FROG missile and its mobile launching platform caught out in the open and destroyed. (B) A missile re-arm vehicle burned to the ground by Air Force jets.

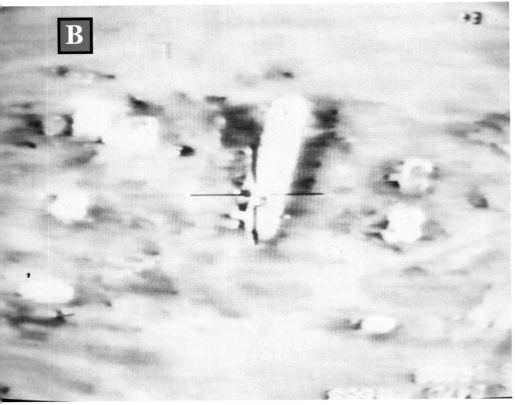

(A) A disabled fuel truck in Iraq, and (B) a Scud TEL targeted by an F-15E. Target identification was often difficult at night, even with the most sophisticated ground and airborne systems.

green hue. By amplifying existing light, human-sized targets can be recognized from almost 100 yards on all but the very darkest nights, with good moonlight extending their range by 50 percent or more. Operating under a last quarter moon, the men can see extremely well, but spotty cloud cover creates sudden, unexpected drops in visibility, in addition to the device's limited peripheral field of vision.

The point man's stubby MP5, night-vision goggles, and modified tactical vest give him an unearthly appearance. Walking behind the point man, the compass man, Staff Sergeant Rodgers, not only navigates with his compass and altimeter, but also by watching his distance count (how far he walks). The team leader occupies the number three position, and his communications man, Sergeant First Class Cranson, holds down number four. Positions five and six are rounded out by the team medic, Master Sergeant Frank Rodrigues, and the demolitions expert, another staff sergeant, who doubles as the patrol's tail gunner. His primary responsibility is to ensure that no one surprises the team from the rear.

While approaching the low ridge where they'll set up their observation post, it becomes painfully clear that they have, indeed, dropped into an area full of Iraqi units. Reaching their destination, the team immediately sets up security, sends out a two-man recon of the area, and digs in.

A Scud missile erect on its launcher and ready to fire.

The troopers are prepared to lie low for days, watching for the elusive Scuds, but dawn quickly reveals that part of Hussein's missile inventory is already operating in this area.

At first, only typical military and civilian traffic can be seen on the east–west highway stretched out before them. It isn't long, though, before Van Hee spots some familiar friends. Tailing along behind a westbound string of civilian Mercedes tractor-trailers is a Ural-375 truck mounting a mobile crane and a pair of Type ZIL-157V tractors hauling elongated cargoes covered by tarps. The vehicles continue for almost two miles and then pull off to the right about a hundred yards into the desert. Excitement runs high and reaches a peak a half hour later when an eight-wheeled MAZ-543 transporter-erector-launcher (a TEL vehicle known to carry Scud missiles) and a ZIL-157V tanker towing a trailer appear to the east. They zoom by and continue on to the other waiting vehicles which, by now, include numerous supply trucks, C^3 vans, and a mix of towed quad 23mm and dual 30mm antiaircraft guns in the process of deploying on both sides of the highway. The top of the TEL is still well covered by sand-colored tarps, but Van Hee is quite certain that it mounts a Scud.

The suspicious TEL remains with the other vehicles for only about 10 minutes before all but the antiaircraft element suddenly begin to move off in column across the desert. After only a few hundred yards, the lead truck turns abruptly to the left into a deep wadi that arches back toward the road passing under it at a long, thin bridge a quarter mile past their original turnoff. As far as the team leader's concerned, this confirms it. There is no reason for an Iraqi unit this far afield to go to this kind of trouble to hide itself unless it's a missile unit. At night, the TEL and select support vehicles will emerge back onto the flat terrain to fire its weapon of terror at Israel.

Sighting through his binoculars, Van Hee begins to list what he sees as the vehicles disappear down the path bulldozed to the dry streambed. As he reels off the NATO names, the team's radio operator writes them on his notepad. After one more sweep of the target area, Van Hee tells Cranson to inform headquarters that the mother of all targets is in front of them. He then slides back into the two-man foxhole, closes his eyes, and tries to relax.

Opening his rucksack flap, Cranson closely examines the satellite communications system (SATCOM). From the outside pocket he pulls a miniature satellite antenna folded so it looks like a small, closed umbrella. Unfolding its legs and arms, Cranson places the device just beyond the lip of the hide hole and checks its frame to ensure that each prong is extended to its maximum position. With a diameter of only 17 inches, the antenna's low profile makes it hard to spot or identify. Cranson plugs the antenna's coaxial cable into the SATCOM and turns it on.

Intense concentration marks the face of a trooper keeping watch on the surrounding terrain from a desert ruin.

While the system hums and ticks through its self-checks and calibrations, the commo man listens through his headset and consults the *Equatorial Satellite Antenna Pointing Guide* for the elevation and azimuth angles required to orient the antenna. Cranson moves the dish back and forth until he hears the unmistakable peep of the orbiting satellite and then settles in to start his transmission. He speaks in slow, distinct tones, sending the entire intelligence picture of what the recon team is viewing to a receiving station in the SOC communications bunker at King Khalid. Immediately, this vital information is passed through the U.S. Air Force liaison officer to CENTCOM's air component tucked away in a basement corner of the Royal Saudi Air Force building in Riyadh.

Within minutes, coalition jets pulled from the Scud-hunting air campaign are vectored from their stations as others scramble from Saudi fields far to the southeast. Twenty-two minutes after the initial report, the first aircraft arrive. The jets briefly circle well out of range of the frustrated Iraqi antiaircraft gunners as they coordinate their attack, and then make straight for the well-camouflaged vehicles parked along the dry streambed.

Tipped off to the Iraqis' exact location, the A-10 Thunderbolt IIs (affectionately called Warthogs, or simply Hogs) turn the wadi into a deathtrap. The jets continuously roll in and pound the missile unit, and then begin to work on targets up and down the highway. Their method of attack seems strange to the hidden team members watching the show with intense interest. All had seen live-fire exercises where the Hog drivers swooped in and plastered targets from treetop heights, but now the Hogs rarely ventured below 8,000 or 10,000 feet to avoid the antiair assets.

Throughout the day, air strikes continue to hit the target-rich environment. Periodic, huge explosions rend the wadi, and Cranson, who is monitoring the Warthogs' communications net, informs Van Hee that the Hog drivers claim "two Scuds TANGO UNIFORM" (tits up—slang for destroyed). Later strikes are conducted almost exclusively by F-16s with some help from Tornado attack aircraft of unknown origin. The team hadn't been briefed that Tornadoes would be in on the show, and although Cranson picks up their cryptic transmissions, he only knows that they are not speaking *American* English.

These aircraft, and all others working the many targets, fly no lower than the Warthogs and, consequently, there are a lot of misses. But Van Hee can clearly see that the cumulative weight of the air attacks has destroyed nearly every vehicle in the area with a combination of rockets, iron bombs, and cluster munitions. The medium-altitude attacks have, moreover, rendered the anti-aircraft guns nearly useless by striking from beyond their effective range. No one in the team sees any coalition aircraft go down.

As evening draws near, the team leader fears that their position is becoming increasingly vulnerable. Although well-hidden on a barely perceptible ridge, they are, nevertheless, located on the highest terrain feature in the area. It might only be a matter of time before the increasingly active Iraqi patrols unearth them. As soon as night falls, the team picks up its gear, sanitizes the area, and heads south across the nearly silent road. Moving carefully, the team settles into a steady, cautious march. Upon reaching a small depression, they form a perimeter and rest before continuing on to the exfiltration point.

But this is as far as they get. Gleason detects the hot thermal images of several trucks pulling off the highway barely 1,500 yards behind them. Both Gleason and Van Hee carry handheld AN/PAS-7 thermal viewers that detect the heat of the vehicles several hundred yards beyond the system's stated range. Almost immediately, the vehicles are joined by a larger semi trailer-sized vehicle. Could it be another Scud TEL? Through their two thermal viewers, the team watches with nervous excitement and glee as what appears to be more Scud launchers and support vehicles roll in. The men believe that their new neighbor is a full-blown battery preparing to launch a nasty surprise at Israel.

Under normal circumstances, the lack of clear, sharp images wouldn't prevent the team from determining if this were a Scud battery. Unfortunately, the recon team not only lacks altitude but is slightly lower than the Iraqis. From their eye-level view, all they can tell is that several dozen vehicles—some quite large—are arrayed to the north.

Whoever they are, the darkness has given them a false sense of security, and Van Hee can make out that they are neither properly dispersed nor making any effort at concealment. The team can easily call in an air strike, but even though the Iraqis are currently not well-dispersed, that could change in an instant. Moreover, if this were a Scud battery, even the fast-movers would have great difficulty identifying the critical launch vehicles, which are almost indistinguishable from fuel trucks and other lengthy vehicles at attack distances. Blanketing the area with cluster bombs wouldn't guarantee the mobile launchers' destruction either, although it would certainly "attrit" their crews and support personnel.

Van Hee simply cannot confirm that the vehicles are what he believes them to be. He instructs Rodrigues and the tail gunner to move toward the highway to get a closer look and gives them his thermal viewer. Gleason watches as their ghostly figures silently disappear. Everyone understands that the men may have to move in as close as 200 or 250 yards before their viewer will let them confirm the team's suspicions. If the approach to the Iraqi unit is difficult, the men might be gone for many hours. During their absence, the team checks and rechecks its equipment and notifies SOC of the situation.

The wait is mercifully short. Helpful terrain features and a surprising lack of security allow the scouts to complete their task in barely three hours. Rodrigues reports that at least two of the mystery vehicles are Scud TELs, and Van Hee wastes no time returning with him to a spot where Rodrigues is confident that the confirmed launchers can be painted for incoming aircraft. When Gleason first spotted the gathering Iraqi vehicles at roughly 1,500 yards, they were beyond the effective range of Van Hee's AN/PAQ-3 MULE target designator, and the laser team would have to travel almost one-third of the way back toward the road to get a clear fix on the TELs. Newer experimental handheld designators that can accurately illuminate targets at roughly three times the distance had recently been sent to the Gulf, but Van Hee's team was not among the lucky few to receive one.

The route back is well known, and the men move with deliberate haste. The midnight hour when Iraq often launches its weapons of terror is fast approaching, and both the laser team and Gleason identify the unmistakable raised pillar of a missile through their thermal viewers.

Rodgers peers intently at the shadowy image of assembled Iraqi vehicles and nervously fingers his M16. From his vantage point, he can see only one other trooper, the tail gunner, about

20 yards to his right, who gives Rodgers a thumbs up. Rodgers knows that he isn't the only man wondering if the fast-movers will make it before the Iraqis launch. He doesn't feel particularly expendable and hopes that the Air Force will refrain from using cluster munitions against close-in ground-lased targets as the team had been briefed before the mission.

Activity suddenly picks up near the road. Several of the smaller Iraqi vehicles scatter in all directions, and a lone dual-30mm antiaircraft gun, positioned slightly east of the launch site, begins to pop green tracers into the air. The team watches, mesmerized from their ringside seats as other antiaircraft artillery, or triple-A, quickly comes to life, sending aloft criss-crossing streams of fire. Cranson, meanwhile, listens in on the approaching jets transmission: "Honey 1, sixty seconds, Maverick . . . Honey 1, ten seconds . . . Honey 1, laser on . . . Spot . . . Honey 1, lock-launch. . . Sixty seconds to laser designator

(Pages 102-104) A surface-to-air recovery (STAR) of two troopers using a Fulton extraction system. An Air Force fast mover drops a canister containing the system—helium bottles, balloon, line, and attached suit. The guard cables and whisker-like probes of an MC-130 yoke open to snare the Fulton's line. Two volunteers with "Are we really going to do this?" looks on their faces are snagged up. The soldiers are hauled aboard through the open rear ramp of the receiving aircraft.

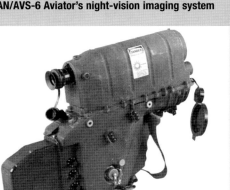
AN/AVS-6 Aviator's night-vision imaging system

Comparative imagery from night vision equipment used by U.S. forces in *Desert Storm*: (top) unaided, daylight photograph of an M606 Jeep and the same vehicle shot from a slightly different angle through (center) image intensification and (bottom) infrared devices.

AN/PVS-7A Night vision goggles

AN/PAQ-3 Modular universal laser equipment (MULE) target designator

AN/PAS-7 Thermal viewer

switch-on . . . Ten seconds to switch-on . . . Laser spot acquired . . . Target locked-on and ordnance fired."

The men have almost grown accustomed to the awe-inspiring spectacle when a huge double explosion bursts skyward. A Maverick air-to-ground missile has slammed into a TEL and ignited its fueled-up weapon.

Most of the triple-A falls silent for what seems like a long time, but one Iraqi gunner recovers from the shock of the explosion almost immediately and resumes shooting even before the fireball disappears into the air. Long strings of triple-A again arch into the sky as Rodgers and the others watch in fascination, knowing that Van Hee is already painting another Scud: "Honey 2, spot . . . Lock-launch . . . Honey 2, terminate. . . Laser spot acquired. . . Target locked on and ordnance fired. . . Have visual contact; laser no longer needed." A second huge explosion lights the scene, and more vehicles scurry away from the carnage. As far as the Iraqi grunts are concerned, all Hussein's little toys do is attract death from above.

Secondary explosions rock the target area as the laser team moves at a steady trot toward the patrol base. The Air Force is holding back from dropping its deadly cluster bombs to give them a jump at getting away from the target. Rodrigues and Van Hee's glowing green images can be clearly seen during their last 100-meter dash to the base, and some of the troopers can't refrain from greeting them with low-volume (*very* low-volume) whoops and hollers as they clear the perimeter. As if to join in the congratulations, the Air Force begins to hit the site again, and now the whole team moves out at a run. The troopers haven't covered a quarter mile when they suddenly smack into an Iraqi squad barely 30 yards away. The Iraqis were apparently on patrol when the air strike erupted and are riding out the attack in this shallow depression.

The startled team comes under fire. Dropping to one knee, Gleason pumps two 9mm rounds into the nearest Iraqi's chest. Without pausing, he switches to the next target, who immediately crumples into a heap, his stomach perforated by two slugs from Gleason's H&K. Immediately sizing up the situation, Van Hee yells for the team to break contact. While moving through their leapfrog maneuver, a lucky round from an RPG-7 shoulder-fired rocket launcher lands between Rodgers and the

Armed and ready, a special operations soldier watches for trouble through his night-vision googles.

Wrapping the staff sergeant in his poncho liner, they gently lay his body into the desert soil. Van Hee carefully checks, then rechecks, the tight ten-digit grid coordinate he has plotted for the unmarked grave and silently swears to his fallen trooper that he'll be back for him. The team says a quick prayer over their friend, and then, carrying Rodgers, they strike out south again. Rodrigues, the team's medic, recognizes that the multiple shrapnel wounds are worse than previously thought. Rodgers is slipping in and out of consciousness and losing blood. Cranson radios the fast FAC that they have a man who will die if they don't get him out soon.

tail gunner. Although most of the explosion is absorbed by the ground, shrapnel rips into Rodgers' right side, and the tail gunner is killed instantly by a dime-sized piece of metal piercing his skull just above the right eye.

The four uninjured troopers immediately lay down an intense base of fire, which convinces the Iraqis to fall back to less dangerous surroundings. The firefight has lasted less than two minutes. One American is dead and another's life is leaking into the rocky earth. Hauling Rodgers and the fallen trooper along with them, the team hurriedly resumes their escape south while Air Force jets strike at Iraqi vehicles streaking pell-mell through the area. The team is in deep, deep trouble, and, if action is not taken quickly, they will either be killed or wind up on the evening news as prisoners of war.

Air–ground communication between the team and SOC is now being maintained by a fast FAC, or forward air controller, who passes word to Cranson that immediate efforts are being initiated to get them out. They are instructed to keep moving south without delay, but they are faced with having to make a decision no soldier wants to make.

The young trooper's body hinders their movement to the extraction point, and they decide to bury him as quickly as possible. In a lonely defile, the team digs a grave for their comrade. It is not very much, as graves go, but they make it with love and respect, and the men dig as deeply as time will permit.

SOC knows that no special operations helicopters are currently available for a quick recovery, nor are there likely to be any until almost mid-morning.

Virtually everything is already committed to the far-flung operations in progress throughout what the Israelis call "Scudinavia" in western Iraq. SOC decides to use an MC-130 Combat Talon equipped with a Fulton Recovery System to conduct a surface-to-air recovery (STAR) of Rodgers. This is not generally a preferred method of extraction because it takes so much time to set up the Fulton and is easily seen, but with helicopter assets unavailable, Rodgers' condition requires it. Alerting the 1st Special Operations Wing, a hasty plan is worked out to recover the wounded DELTA trooper.

The Extractions

Arar Royal Military Airfield near Banadah is the launch site of some of Operation *Desert Storm*'s most inventive missions. It's not an unusual place to find one or two of the 1st Special Operations Wing's MC-130s, and when the call comes down, immediate preparations are made for the STAR. First, a modified delivery canister is loaded with all the items needed by the team to set up the recovery. The canister is then affixed to the waiting A-10's weapons pylon, and the Warthog is immediately launched toward western Iraq. As the "Sandy"* Hog driver and his wingman speed north, the crew of the MC-130 receives their mission brief. Not uncharacteristically, the crew takes the briefing quite professionally; yet, underneath their calm exterior, adrenaline surges. They are about to execute a mission that they have trained hard for, a mission that has not been performed in combat for nearly 20 years.

Already deep in the desert, the recon team is now told to move beyond their original pickup point into an even more desolate area well away from any known military targets. After several hours, the exhausted team comes upon a group of ruined dwellings and sets up defensive positions as dawn begins to break. Rodrigues has just changed Rodgers' i.v. and is connecting a new bag of saline solution when Cranson's radio crackles to life. The Sandy pilot is attempting to contact the team. Hopefully, it will appear to any nearby Iraqis that the Hog driver and his wingman are out hunting for targets of opportunity and will avoid any curious overtures.

Van Hee is informed that he should mark their position for a "delivery." Using a mirror, Van Hee signals his location to the Sandys performing their lazy search pattern well away from the team. After receiving an acknowledgment from the pilot, Van Hee moves out about 175 yards from the perimeter, places a single orange panel in the gravel, and immediately moves back to the shelter of the ruins. The pair of Warthogs are continuing their indirect meander toward the ruins when they spot a group of Iraqi trucks moving parallel to the team approximately two miles out. Although they do not appear to be looking for the troopers, the Sandys take no chances and proceed to spoil the Iraqis' morning with fire from their 30mm Gatling nose cannons. As the Hogs leave the burning vehicles, they approach the ruins indirectly by flying in a low, wide arc that, hopefully, won't draw attention to the hidden Americans. No extra passes are made over the site, and the equipment canister is pickled off as the ugly jets roar overhead.

Thirty minutes behind the Sandys, the MC-130 Combat Talon penetrates into enemy territory. While passing over the berm line, the special operations aircraft receives an ominous radio report from the E-3A Sentry orbiting in Saudi airspace behind them. Electronic warfare officers operating the AWACS' sophisticated sensors detect a number of hostile radar impulses. Despite the fact that the Air Force owns the sky, being painted over Iraqi territory always causes concern. Most of the Talon's crew had friends on the ill-fated AC-130 Specter gunship that failed to get out of Kuwaiti airspace when locked on by a surface-

to-air missile. The result was charred debris floating in the Gulf and no survivors.

As the Talon closes on the team's location, Van Hee and Gleason open the canister. Extracting its contents, they find a balloon, nylon line, harness, and suit along with a bottle of helium. Rodrigues checks Rodgers' condition while Van Hee and Gleason prepare to inflate the balloon, and Cranson makes contact with the inbound Talon. Not only is the MC-130 approaching, but the pair of A-10s continue to ply the area in ostensibly random patterns, and a flight of F-16s has already assumed a guardian-angel role well to the east but within easy striking distance if trouble develops. The Warthogs again cruise past the ruins while Van Hee and Gleason affix the helium bottle to the balloon that will stretch Rodgers' life-line in reach of the specially equipped rescue aircraft. As it inflates, the bulbous cream and silver balloon takes on the shape of a giant fish, its floppy fins growing firmer with each passing second.

Rodrigues and Cranson gingerly ease Rodgers into the olive-green recovery suit sewn firmly to the Fulton's harness. As its fur-lined hood is placed around Rodgers' face, his glazed eyes open slightly to Rodrigues' familiar grin. His medic friend has been in DELTA for a long time and has a well-earned reputation as a battlefield doctor. Patting Rodgers' thigh, he says with a chuckle, "You gonna go on a neat ride, my man. It's up, up, and away for you." Rodrigues does his best to put up a brave front for his buddy but fears that Rodgers may have lost too much blood. His face is gray and expressionless, but it seems for a moment that he tries to acknowledge what the medic is saying.

Twenty minutes from the pickup, the balloon creeps slowly skyward. It reaches its full height, and Rodgers sits securely attached to its tether while the team, minus the doc, stands guard in a circle resembling a herd of buffaloes shielding a wounded calf. Rodrigues continues his lively chatter to help keep his patient awake and gently pats and strokes his uninjured left arm. Although Rodgers doesn't know it, the determined woofing is paying off, and he dimly comprehends that his buddies are doing everything they can for him.

At 525 feet, the balloon acts as a beacon for all to see and is the reason that the team had to put so much distance between themselves and the highway. The incoming MC-130's unusual nose now resembles a snout with two large whiskers, which are actually probes swung outward to form the yoke. Their main function is to guide the line into place at the center of the nose as the plane makes the pickup.

Cautiously lining up on the balloon, the pilot throttles the airplane down to 112, 105, then only 97 knots for the pickup

*An A-10 pilot specially trained for rescue escort (RESCORT) missions. The rugged A-10's ability to loiter for extended periods of time makes it perfect for conducting searches in a high-threat environment, and Sandys are experts at locating survivors. By marking target locations and suppressing enemy fire, they allow more vulnerable rescue aircraft to do their job. The term originated during the Vietnam War as a call sign used by A-1E Skyraider pilots providing gunfire suppression during rescue operations.

The venerable A-10 Thunderbolt II "Warthog" and Delta formed a deadly Scud hunter-killer team in Iraq. The A-10s also proved themselves to be effective search-and-rescue assets in Iraq.

As the MC-130 speeds toward friendly airspace, the remainder of the recon team moves out. A well-timed air operation, centered mainly along the highway to the north, is initiated by the F-16s and a fresh pair of A-10s to mask their movement, and the troopers head south by southwest toward a new pickup point several miles away. Although appropriate helicopter assets will be available in a few hours, SOC has decided to wait until dark to make the extraction, since Rodgers has been rescued and the recon team is in no immediate danger.

The team members had flung their hide-site covers into their foxholes and buried them when they sanitized their original position, but the rough terrain they're now moving into offers many opportunities for natural concealment. They soon come upon a wadi that offers a reasonable amount of security and decide that it will suffice till nightfall. After the midnight firefight, Hussein's forces know that American commandos are in the area, but ongoing airstrikes have given the Iraqis plenty of other things to worry about, and their movement has been heavily restricted for scores of miles in all directions.

The only enemy assaulting the men is a determined legion of sandfleas, which tirelessly press their attack. They do, however, also receive periodic visits from various Air Force jets. The pilots make it a point to fly close enough to the Delta team to scout for hostile forces, yet their seemingly random passes are conducted at varied-enough intervals to give no clue to the whereabouts of the hidden soldiers.

Night comes quickly and the temperature drops like a stone even before the sun disappears from the horizon. As the four men make their final equipment checks before moving out, help is crossing the Saudi–Iraq border 100 miles to the southeast. Boring through the gathering fog at 60 feet off the ground, a lone MH-60 Black Hawk is finally on its way to retrieve the soldiers.

Almost 10 hours have passed since Rodgers was extracted, and Van Hee's team starts to move south again. The welcome night engulfs the dirty, unshaven troopers, and their night-vision goggles allow them to move with the assurance of prowling nocturnal beasts unencumbered by darkness.

In spite of the sophisticated NVGs and their apparent isolation, the desert holds one more surprise. As they near the pickup point, a young goat herder casually emerges from a depression 40 yards to their right. Upon seeing the ghost-like

and aims at the target area marked on the nylon rope by three orange streamers. Striking the target markers, the probes guide the line to the yoke and secure it as the plane flies over the Delta team. With a minimum of fanfare, Rodgers is snatched from the ground and becomes a small dot hurtling behind the Talon. While the STAR is a nerve-racking affair for the soldiers to watch, they know that Rodgers actually experiences less of a jolt during the pickup than he did when he opened his parachute.

In the gaping cargo bay, the loadmaster and crew chief now prepare to winch their human cargo on board. The nylon line is pressed firmly against the Talon's belly by the rush of air, and inside the bay, the crew chief and loadmaster move quickly to hook it, much as one snaps a fishing line. Reeling in the line and attaching it to the Talon's internal hydraulic winch, the precious cargo is slowly drawn into the cargo bay. Soon, Rodgers is in the safety of the aircraft while Air Force Reserve trauma specialists work frantically to stabilize him.

An E-3A Sentry at Dhahran, Saudi Arabia.

apparitions, he runs screaming through the darkness, scattering livestock in all directions. Fearing a return of Iraqi soldiers, the team moves through the area quickly and sets up a defensive perimeter 600 yards from their encounter. Speaking in hushed tones with the inbound chopper, Van Hee guides the bird in until the troopers can be seen on its infrared imager.

As the Black Hawk's wheels touch the hard-packed dirt, the remaining four troopers scramble aboard and slide across the metal floor plates to hold each other in an embrace only those who have faced the ultimate challenge know. "We made it!" Gleason yells above the pitch of the engines as the helicopter begins to rise above the desert floor.

After looking out of the waist gunner's hatch for any signs of Iraqi forces, Van Hee wearily leans back and says, "Christ, I hope so."

The Final Manifest Call
Epilogue to the First Edition

Along Ardennes Road, framed by a stand of regal North Carolina pines, the John F. Kennedy Special Warfare Center Chapel occupies a place of dignity and serenity. Against the hustle and organized chaos that characterizes this sprawling airborne post, it provides a safe haven of sanity and peace whether the visitor is a regular churchgoer or just passing through.

Framed against the gathering clouds of an incoming spring rain, a memorial service is taking place. It is a closed service to avoid the prying eyes of newspaper reporters still trying to write stories about *Desert Storm*. Although the service was unannounced, the chapel is crowded. Word has passed quickly around the special operations community that one of their own is being remembered today. Conspicuous in their off-the-rack suits, cowboy boots, and nonregulation mustaches and haircuts, the members of a DELTA troop have gathered once more. Along with their wives, they are here to help the young widow weather one more storm. It is a unique scene—one that rarely occurred in the past few years but has often been repeated since the operations "over there."

The widow's five-year-old son, sandy blond hair neatly combed and out of character, sits on the edge of his front-row seat. Gently poking an imagined spot on the chapel's maroon carpet with the toe of his Sunday best, he absently wonders, not quite knowing or understanding why he is here. He is aware that his mom's world is in disarray, and her sadness is something he has never seen before. All he knows is that the man whose

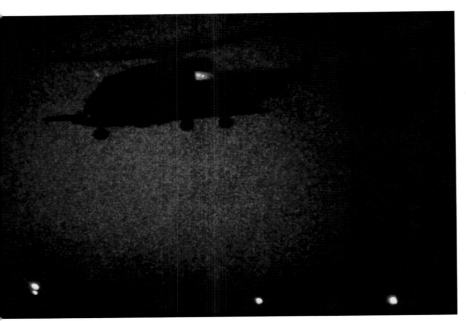

A special operations helicopter streaking at low level across the night sky.

zled old warrior remembers similar services after *Desert I*, *Urgent Fury*, *Just Cause*, and drifts back to the days before he left Smoke Bomb Hill to join DELTA at the old stockade. His thoughts go back to the Green Beret Parachute Club, its cold beer, warm friendships, and the old jukebox nestled in the corner next to the pool tables. He smiles to himself as he remembers that one song, a song from an unpopular war that saw so many of the special operations community answer the requirements of the ultimate test. Though not all DELTA troopers were initially special forces–qualified, most ended with that qualification, and an old war song expressed best the thoughts and feelings of this moment: "Her Green Beret has met his fate."

It's not all glory and gunsmoke in the realm of special operations—especially in covert operations. Boredom spans months, and then moments of sheer gut-wrenching, piss-in-your-pants horror strike out of the blue. But that's what they signed up for. No yellow ribbons, no victory parades, no grand celebrations would greet these secret warriors. Just a gentle hug, a kind word, or a pat on the back that seemed to say, "Well done." That, and, "Clean up your gear and get ready for the next one!"

And there *will* be a next one—somewhere, sometime. And odds are that DELTA will be used not as it was during Iraq's stinging defeat, but in its traditional counterterrorist role.

For over a quarter of a century, the former Soviet Union and its surrogates in Eastern Europe, Latin America, and the Middle East gave safe haven to the world's most dangerous international terrorists. The collapse of Soviet communism, coupled with the shutting off of terrorist's revenue by oil-rich Persian Gulf states angered over their backing of Iraq, have left terrorist organizations in disarray. Increasingly isolated politically and cut off from training and supplies from Europe and money from the Gulf, they bicker among themselves over how best to satisfy their grudge against the West and any Middle Eastern government unappreciative of their past deeds. They are, to put it bluntly, out of work and out of cash.

But the breather this has given the West is likely to be short-lived. As the world speeds toward the twenty-first century, it finds itself with more wild cards in its deck of nations. The familiar bipolar dominance of the United States and the former Soviet Union is gone for good, as the evil empire disintegrates into numerous successor states of ques-

picture occupies the table in front of the chapel is not coming home. His father left home late one night "on business." That was not an unusual occurrence in his young life, but now a new twist has occurred. Mom said that his best friend has gone to live with God forever.

His father's friends, gathered around the family in a supportive ring, knew the story all too well. The smiling young soldier, pictured with the coveted green beret, had been their friend, and in this close-knit group of professionals, that one word, *friend*, was all that required their loyalty.

The emotion of these men was not a complicated show. Each behaved simply but with a degree of maturity in combat that comes only to a veteran. They accepted what was thrown their way, hiding their hatred, fear, confusion, and pride behind the mantle of a well-trained special operations soldier. To this group and the many others like them, the specter of death was always a member of the team. In this particular case, their friend was no longer able to avoid death's embrace. Thousands of miles away, hidden in an unmarked grave deep in Iraq's rugged western province, their trusted friend and the young boy's father had rested until a subsequent team, under Gary Van Hee, recovered his lifeless form.

As the chaplain exhorts the group not to grieve but to pray for the Great Jumpmaster's protection of their comrade's soul, people's thoughts drift to other places, other actions, and other services. And the veterans of *Desert Storm* reflect on the madness of the previous few weeks.

Hanging back a little from the rest of the mourners, a griz-

tionable stability. These new countries are, themselves, not homogeneous entities and are likely to be rent by factional fighting in the decade to come. They are also the inheritors of at least 27,000 nuclear weapons. Despite pronouncements of their good intentions, their desperate need for hard currency and sporadic control of their own territory may result in some leakage of nuclear weapons or, more likely, nuclear materials and production expertise into the hands of terrorists.

This threat to peace and a ghastly new form of warfare— environmental terrorism—may also cause elite counterterrorist units like DELTA to retool their operational methods. The sight of massive oil slicks released in the Persian Gulf and black clouds boiling up from oil fires to shut off the noonday sun will not be lost on the next generation of would-be terrorists. Moreover, their twisted logic will lead some terrorists to use the results of *Desert Storm* to add fuel to whatever cause they favor.

Dozens of captured Palestinian and Shiite terrorists have been dumped into this

A soldier is laid to rest.

cauldron of change, let loose by the Iraqis when they invaded Kuwait or released by the Israelis as part of the package deal that freed a handful of Western hostages. Like the wandering freelance warriors of feudal Japan who traded their violent skills for gold and fame, these modern-day *ronin* are available to any would-be despot or group fanning the flames of ethnic or religious unrest across Europe, Asia, and the Middle East. Key terrorist networks remain intact, and a number of groups and individuals dropped from sight when the vigilance of America's intelligence assets was directed to combat in the Gulf. Now that the flex of security operations has fallen to its normal lull, the specter of terrorists finding new work in the developing chaos is very real, and Americans abroad are, as always, notoriously easy targets for any group desiring big headlines.

The pros of DELTA are ready.

Chapter 7

The '90s: SAME THREAT —NEW FACES

War is the continuation of politics by other means.
—Mao Tse-Tung, "On Protracted War," 1938

War is not the continuation of policy. It is the breakdown of policy.
—Hans von Seekt, Thoughts of a Soldier, 1930

A force of special operators (DELTA, Rangers, and SOAR) practice for a search-and-seize mission at a Fort Bragg training site.

The 1990s was a busy decade for DELTA. The unit received numerous upgrades in equipment to help fix the deficiencies exposed during the Scud hunt in Iraq. The SOT became the beneficiary of many enhancements to its already state-of-the-art equipment, such as more realistic targets and special cameras for low-light resolution. New training scenarios were also developed for situations that the squadrons would inevitably face.

Former DELTA officers also rose to prominence within the special operations community during this period. Chief among them was Peter J. Schoomaker, a DELTA squadron commander from 1978 to 1981 and 1985 to 1988, he occupied the unit's top slot from 1989 through 1992 and rose to command the most senior and demanding Army and joint special operations billets before retiring in 2000. Because of his unique experience, abilities, and his deep understanding of the Army's future needs in the global war on terror, Schoomaker was pulled from his well-earned retirement to become U.S. Army chief of staff in 2003.

Personal protection and liaison duties remained a priority during the 1990s, and DELTA continued to provide backup for federal, state, and local agencies at select high-profile events that might prove tempting to terrorists. The security force for one such event, the 1996 Olympics in Atlanta, was the largest U.S. peacetime security operation ever conducted. (Although much larger numbers of DELTA troopers were available for the 2005 presidential inauguration ceremonies, it was arguably a "wartime" contingency.) There was also no shortage of world conflicts where the National Command Authority called on DELTA's services.

Operation *Amber Star*

The Dayton Peace Accord was signed in 1995, ending a three-year civil war in the former Yugoslavia that left half a million dead, and the checkerboard of Serbian and Bosnian areas in Bosnia-Herzegovina settled into a wary peace under the control of IFOR (Implementing Force) troops. When the larger, heavier Stabilization Force (SFOR) later entered these areas, DELTA and British SAS personnel led the way as covert reconnaissance units. Additional missions assigned to DELTA personnel included providing support as part of the World Courts' security force, capturing and securing suspected war criminals for transport to The Hague for trial. DELTA operatives were part of the task force supporting Operation *Amber Star* in 1997 with

missions specifically targeting the Serb leader Radovan Karadzic. They and their intelligence support element, ISA, also entered target areas in search of persons indicted for war crimes (PIFWCs) and to monitor the movements of other suspected war criminals.

Code Name *Centra Spike*

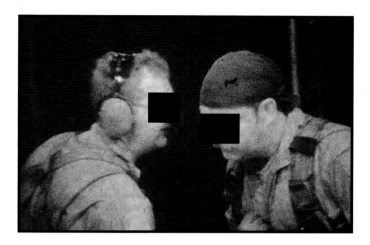

Trooper and Combat Talon crew chief prepare for a night Fulton recovery mission.

Pablo Escobar rose to prominence in 1983 as one of the strongest members of Colombia's drug cartels. So vicious and brazen were his activities and those of the other cartels that they soon gave rise to the term narco-terrorism. The foundation for the term was the alliance forged by Escobar's murderous Medellin Cartel and the Marxist guerrillas operating with near impunity in the cocaine-producing areas of Colombia. In 1989, the Colombian government requested special operations assistance from the United States, and ISA personnel initiated operations under code name *Centra Spike*. DELTA troopers entered the picture in 1992 as "advisors" to the Colombians, and Escobar's violent death in December 1992 is surrounded by rumors that DELTA snipers were directly involved in the takedown. However, there is little evidence to support this contention.

Operation *Uphold Democracy*

In the early 1990s, the Caribbean island of Hispaniola was again a focal point of violence. A military junta ousted Haiti's first freely elected president Jean-Bertrand Aristide and, together

A Somali gunman of warlord Mohamed Farrah Aidid sprints to a new firing position among scurrying children who act as cover for his tactical movements.

with remnants of the *ton-ton macoutes* secret police, suppressed Aristide's supporters. An agreement was reached that the junta would relinquish power, but a U.S. Navy ship carrying the initial elements of Joint Task Force Haiti Assistance was threatened and forced to withdraw from the Haitian capital, Port au Prince, in October 1993. Several high-ranking Americans, including Colin Powell and former president Jimmy Carter, as well as United Nations officials were sent to Haiti in late 1994 and 1995 to initiate negotiations for the peaceful entry of a U.S. stabilization force and to assess election preparations. The accompanying personal security detail (PSD) was comprised of DELTA troopers, including marksmen.

Lima Takedown

In 1996, the Japanese ambassador's residence in Peru was seized by terrorists during a large diplomatic reception. The Peruvians conducted the operation to free the hostages, which included foreign ambassadors and senior Peruvian officials, with their own CT forces. Peruvian special forces had received training from U.S. special operations mobile training teams, and additional support during the operation was provided by DELTA

advisors. An SAS team was also sent to Lima because of the presence of diplomatic personnel among the hostages. The embassy takedown was successful.

Operation *Allied Force*

DELTA troopers were deployed to support the NATO move into Kosovo in 1998—Operation *Allied Force*. According to sources close to the operation, DELTA assets were tasked to collect intelligence on Serbian command centers and armored units. When the NATO air campaign was initiated, DELTA was on call to quickly rescue any downed pilots captured by the Serbs. An additional mission was to be prepared to conduct snatch operations against individuals on the World Court's expanding list of most-wanted war criminals, including Serbian president Slobodan Milosevic.

Taking a Knife to a Gunfight— Operation *Irene*

While most DELTA missions in the 1990s were of the just-doing-business variety, the repercussions of one operation had an impact every bit as profound as the disaster at *Desert I*.

As noted in Chapter 2, the exploits of Germany's GSG-9 in October 1977 occupies a rightful place on lists of successful operations. But the location of their mission—Mogadishu, Somalia—will also be remembered for another operation where, despite uncommon valor and sheer guts, the cost of success was far too high. Like so many other American military actions, the Battle of Mogadishu (also called the Battle of the Black Sea) would again signify the bravery, professionalism, and dedication of the individual special operator.

The United States entered the swirling insanity of Somalia's civil war in December 1992 with Operation *Restore Hope*. Under President Bill Clinton's new administration, a multinational UN force assumed control of operations in a "stabilized" Somalia in May 1993.

Enter "General" Mohamed Farrah Aidid, chairman of a faction within the Hawiye clan's political party and the tribal warlord of the Habar Gidir sub-clan in southern Mogadishu. Aidid's continual efforts to destabilize the humanitarian mission, and his intertribal warfare, culminated in an ambush that left 24 Pakistani peacekeepers dead and a bomb detonation that killed four U.S. solders. In only a few months, the situation in Mogadishu had again nose-dived into chaos.

The media-savvy warlord had clearly initiated combat operations against UN/U.S. forces, and President Clinton decided that Aidid needed to be permanently removed from the television screen. With no prior experience in this type of conflict, Clinton and his senior defense and state department chiefs rushed into the same trap that ensnared former President Lyndon Johnson in the 1960s. He tried to run a war from the White House.

Task Force Ranger (TFR), composed principally of Special Operations Forces, was deployed to Mogadishu in late August 1993. TFR staff officers soon found themselves besieged—not by Somali militiamen—but by "command guidance" from Washington targeting Aidid and his top commanders for snatch-and-scoot operations. Several missions were executed, but most made little or no progress. Intelligence operatives, however, did provide the special operations planners with a target, and Operation *Irene* was hatched.

Additional firepower was critical to this operation. The available force would not be able to use darkness to offset their smaller numbers (as they normally did). After a detailed mission analysis, Joint Special Operations Command (JSOC) planners recommended—and the commander requested—increased backup in the form of armored personnel carriers and tank support. These assets would be used for the extraction

One of the two crash sites in Mogadishu where special operations personnel and aircraft where lost during the battle.

phase of the operation, and provide assets for a quick reaction force (QRF).

Clinton and his senior advisors did not want it to appear that the U.S. was increasing its military presence in Africa and were concerned that adding heavy forces would send the wrong signal. But they didn't understand that overwhelming force was required. Secretary of Defense Les Aspin reportedly went along with the crowd although he knew the ground commanders should be in control. Lower down the chain of command it was also decided to withhold AC-130 Specter gunships from the operation.

Task Force Ranger (TFR) was given the mission of capturing key Aidid lieutenants Omar Salad and Mohamed Hassan Awale in a combination air–mobile and ground operation converging on their hideout near Mogadishu's Bakkara Market.

The plan called for 1st SFOD- DELTA (A) and SEAL Team Six attachments to fast-rope rappel, then search, capture, and secure the high-value targets (HVT), while providing inner security. Company B, 3rd Battalion, 75th Ranger Regiment (Airborne), provided the muscle. Rangers would fast-rope rappel, and then secure a square perimeter on four corners of the operation's target area while other Rangers, using vehicles, conducted the extraction operation of air–mobile force and high-value targets (HVT) from the target area.

The 160th SOAR (A) was to provide air support for the infiltration, assault, and exfiltration of the TFR ground convoy using MH-6, AH-6, fast-rope-capable MH-60, and UH-60 command and control-capable airframes. After-action reports and interviews with participants indicate that the air–mobile

DELTA snipers Master Sergeant Gary Gordon (A) and Sergeant First Class Randy Shughart (B) earned the first Medal of Honors awarded since the Vietnam War for actions above and beyond the call of duty when saving the life of SOAR pilot Michael Durant in Mogadishu. DELTA troopers Timothy Martin, Earl Fillmore, and Daniel Busch also made the supreme sacrifice during the mission, and team leader Sergeant First Class Matthew Rierson was killed several days later by a mortar round. Said Durant "Without a doubt, I owe my life to these two men and their bravery. . . . Those guys came in when they had to know it was a losing battle. There was nobody else left to back them up. If they had not come in, I wouldn't have survived." The events of this mission have been well documented in the book and movie *Black Hawk Down*. In 1996, the U.S. Navy named two ships after Shughart and Gordon. At Fort Polk's Joint Readiness Training Center (JRTC), the largest town inside of "The Box" is named "Shughart-Gordon." *(B) Courtesy parents of Randy Shugart and www.jenmartinez.com.*

force and ground convoy was composed of approximately 180 personnel, 14 vehicles, and 20 helicopters.

The 10th Mountain Division's 14th Infantry Regiment readied a quick-reaction force (QRF) to assist the extraction if Task Force Ranger ran into trouble. Initially company-sized, events would necessitate that the QRF use all of the regiment's 2nd Battalion and the division's AH-1 attack helicopters.

Joint Task Force Command Center (Forward) would be located with the airborne command and control with all TFR elements monitoring the command frequency. Operational support including medical evacuation would follow standard operating procedures for what was planned to be a quick snatch of some bad guys.

The assault force operators approached their target and, as their aircraft lined up for the final approach, code words to execute the operation were transmitted over all communications nets. "Irene, Irene, Irene" was clearly heard, sending Rangers and DELTA troopers fast roping into their objectives.

This was the last part of the operation to follow the plan.

Anyone who's been in combat knows that a plan is only good until the bullets start to fly! A Ranger was seriously injured when he lost his grip while fast roping and ended up in a crum-pled heap below the chopper. But the chopper was also in serious trouble as shoulder-fired rocket-propelled grenades hurtled past the cockpits and open troop doors.

As the assault force searched for their captives, an MH-60 was hit by an RPG-7 and crashed into the street below. The alarm "Black Hawk down!" was heard across the communications net. The extraction force wasn't doing much better. The vehicles were being delayed by local militia and civilians who were erecting obstacles and barricades and igniting tires in an effort to block the extraction team. As the vehicles were slowed or halted, the convoy was assaulted by rocks, AK47 fire, and then RPGs.

The majority of the assault force, having observed the crash of the MH-60, initiated a rescue effort that quickly turned into a major gun fight. More than 90 Rangers and DELTA operators were effectively pinned down at the crash site by the local militia, whose ranks swelled to several thousand.

Then a second MH-60, call sign Super 64, was downed. The pilot and only survivor of the crash was Chief Warrant Officer Mike Durant, and his situation was perilous at best. Super 64 had crashed in full view of the marketplace, and an angry Somali mob was approaching the crash site. Flying overhead, two DELTA snipers, Master Sergeant Gary Gordon and Sergeant First Class Randy Shughart saw the impending danger as they aimed fire on the well-armed mob. After numerous radio calls requesting permission to assist Durant, they were finally permitted to be inserted and move to the injured pilot's side.

Shughart and Gordon took up defensive positions to protect Durant against the Somali mob. Armed with a ridged stock MP5 and an M1A/M14, these two soldiers took on the crowd. The Somali militiamen shielded themselves with willing women and children to try to prevent the Americans from returning fire. The 7.62 Gatling guns wreaked a vengeance like none before, but everyone's best efforts couldn't save the men from the angry mob. Mike Durant, the lone survivor, was taken hostage while the stripped, mutilated bodies of his protectors were dragged before the TV cameras.

Throughout the night, the assault force and part of the QRF beat off attacks by the militia. At daylight, they fought their way out with the invaluable assistance of a Malaysian force of armored personnel carriers, and evacuated to a nearby Pakistani compound.

Aftermath

Operation *Irene* extracted a high cost in human life. Eighteen Americans and two Malaysians perished, and some 78 Americans, seven Malaysians, and two Pakistanis were wounded. Based in analytical results from the gunship tapes, an estimated 700 to 1,000 Somalis were wounded and 300 died. Losses to Aidid's forces were so severe that he was never able to extend his control beyond southern Mogadishu. He was ousted as the leader of his own political faction and died as a result of gunshot wounds in 1995.

The failure to provide tanks and armored personnel carriers was costly to the Clinton administration. As the nation's commander in chief, Clinton demanded that the on-the-ground commander take full responsibility—in writing—for the failure of the operation. This ax fell on the commander of the special operations task force, Brigadier General William Garrison, who followed orders and wrote the letter. But according to reliable sources, someone in the special operations community exacted a degree of revenge. The letter was delivered to the White House—along with an edited version of the "best" gunship footage. Sources indicated that there were green faces and queasy stomachs at the White House after viewing the tape.

An AH-1 Cobra gunship returns fire on Somali gunman.

A patrol moves through the close confines of Mogadishu's Bakara Market.

For their sacrifices on October 3, 1993, Sergeant First Class Randall D. Shughart and Master Sergeant Gary L. Gordon were awarded of the Medal of Honor. They were the first members of DELTA to be so honored and were the first recipients of the award since the Vietnam War. President Clinton presented the medals to their next of kin and offered his hand to Shughart's father at the conclusion of the ceremony. Standing tall, and looking the commander in chief in the eye, Mr. Shughart refused his outstretched hand and said, "You are not fit to be president." When tracked down later by a *Wall Street Journal* reporter, Mrs. Shughart said that the president offered no reply.

Mr. and Mrs. Shughart turned and left the reception.

Chapter 8

AFGHANISTAN AND IRAQ

Now I shall go far and far into the north, playing the Great Game. . . .
—Rudyard Kipling, 1901

In the aftermath of al Qaeda's 9/11 attack, a piece of the World Trade Center hangs precariously after sheering down through a building across the street. *FEMA*

Since the time of Peter the Great, numerous nations and adventurers, traders, soldiers, explorers, intelligence agents, and spies, have ranged over Central Asia in what Kipling referred to as "the Great Game." In October 2001, as a result of the September 11 terrorist attacks in New York and Washington, D.C., the world—and more specifically Afghanistan—was introduced to the American version of this time-honored exercise.

U.S. forces learned many important tactical and operational lessons in Mogadishu, but the shadowy, well-financed al Qaeda terrorist organization led by Osama bin Laden came away with its own "lesson learned." Bin Laden maintained in interviews and communiqués that the quick American withdrawal from Somalia proved that the United States was far weaker than the Soviet Union, which fought for years in Afghanistan before calling it quits. The weak—sometimes nonexistent—military responses to al Qaeda's increasingly deadly bombings against Americans in the Middle East and Africa did nothing to disabuse him of this notion.

Al Qaeda agents and the Taliban militia, which supplied them a secure base of operations in Afghanistan, quickly learned after the bombing of American embassies in Africa, the U.S. compound at Khobar Towers in Saudi Arabia, and the USS *Cole* in Yemen, that they had finally gone too far on 9/11. Americans suddenly woke up to the fact that they were at war. A special operations team member in Afghanistan neatly summarized Americans' reaction, "Don't piss in the wind, don't sword fight with Zorro, and do not piss off the United States of America and George Bush!"

Military operations in the region fell under the direct control of the U.S. Central Command (CENTCOM). Unlike in Somalia, the White House did not interfere while appropriate forces were shifted to the region as quickly as possible. CENTCOM's rapid introduction and integration of special operations and paramilitary specialists with conventional assets, such as B-52 bombers and Navy attack aircraft, had a far-reaching and devastating impact on the architects of the September 11 attacks.

DELTA's participation in Operation *Enduring Freedom* began with their arrival at a base known simply as K2. This not-so-covert installation was an old Soviet air base just north of the Afghan border in Uzbekistan. It was also the headquarters of Task Force Dagger, as the teams principally from 5th Special Forces Group (Airborne) were known.

DELTA's retaliation for 9/11 began on the night of October 19 as part of the newly formed Task Force 11, which was created to target suspected or known terrorists and eliminate them through snatches, capture, or other means. They conducted an air–mobile raid and takedown of a Taliban compound near Kandahar, and although they gathered some intelligence, their primary target, Commander of the Faithful Mullah Mohammed Omar, could not be found. Omar, a long-time friend and reputed father-in-law of bin Laden, was the guiding force behind the Taliban's strict interpretation of Islamic law and use of Afghani territory under his control for al Qaeda training and staging facilities. A significant fight ensued, and DELTA was reported to have sustained heavy casualties but no deaths.

The swift, violent war conducted against al Qaeda and Taliban forces in Afghanistan saw the use of the full range of special operations techniques and procedures. The close cooperation of the many special operations units (foreign and domestic) can only lead the student of unconventional warfare to recognize this theater of operations as a special operators' paradise.

But on November 25, 2001, the paradise erupted into a living hell. Thousands of detainees were held at the ancient fortress of Qala-i-Jangi, where the basics of how to segregate and handle unpredictable prisoners of war were carelessly cast aside. Al Qaeda operatives, Taliban militia, Islamic volunteers from Pakistan, Iraq, Iran, Saudi Arabia, along with Chechen, Somali,

During preparations for a night resupply operation in Afghanistan, a special operator has to shout over the roar of an MC-130's engines to be heard.

The flight engineer of an MH-53M prepares for a search-and-rescue mission during operations against al Qaeda and the Taliban. The "Pave Low stinger" by his side is a 7.62mm minigun.

and Western—including American—fighters took over the prison. An ad hoc force, consisting of every friendly element within driving distance, had to first contain, then retake Qala-i-Jangi the hard way—one brick at a time. The friendlies included DELTA, SAS, special forces, CIA operatives, and some 10th Mountain Division troops, along with Northern Alliance soldiers and militiamen. Nearly 500 Taliban and al Qaeda operatives were killed in the three-day battle.

With bin Laden's escape from Afghanistan and the appearance of one of his chief lieutenants, Ayman al-Zarqawi, in Baghdad, America turned its sites on Saddam Hussein's Iraq. Even before al-Zarqawi's arrival from Afghanistan, Hussein had long harbored arch-murderer Abu Nidal in Baghdad, and was now supplying funds not only to Hammas and the PLO, but also to families of Palestinian suicide bombers in Israel. A sworn enemy of the Unites States who invaded two of his neighbors and fired intermediate-range ballistic missiles at two others, who used poison gas against Iran and his own Kurdish citizens, Hussein's power and standing in the Muslim world was clearly on the rise. With UN sanctions imposed after the Gulf War steadily unraveling and soon to leave

him free to expand or restart his weapons programs, the Bush administration decided to preempt the threat by removing Hussein and his regime from power.

Going Downtown

After a frenzied deployment to the Gulf, troopers settled into a boring daily routine at B Squadron's forward operating base near Kuwait City. Dressed in sterile (no identifying name tags or unit patches) desert battle dress uniforms and desert boots, the squadron's teams practiced close-quarter battle, zeroed weapons, and prepared to take the battle to Saddam Hussein and his followers.

At 1400 hours, Chief Warrant Officer John McAlister's businesslike stride indicated that something was brewing. Known as Big Mac because of his fondness for hamburgers, McAlister had just returned from a briefing with the operations and intelligence staff section. Settling lightly on an olive drab cot, he directed the team to gather 'round.

"We have received a warning order for a mission tomorrow night," Mac said, as he slowly canvassed the faces of his team.

Without referring to his notes, McAlister briefly laid out the broad plan. The team would infiltrate into Baghdad, support the Air Force with laser guidance of smart munitions against a high-value target, conduct battle damage assessment, and exfiltrate.

The remainder of the team's time was spent in preparation, briefings, and rehearsals. Each man was prescribed a load that is constantly updated and reduced to the required items needed for the mission. The operators would infiltrate wearing dark soccer warm-up suits, running shoes, and no head gear. With their beards, mustaches, and warm-ups (like many young Iraqis wear), the team would be able to blend in.

Each man would carry an A-III assault pack loaded with compasses, first-aid kits, communications equipment, high-energy rations, ammunition, windbreakers, and water in CamelBak bladders. Carefully packed in one assault pack was an enhanced version of the Special Operations Forces laser marker (SOFLAM), far superior to the MULE target designator used by DELTA in the 1991 Gulf War. After the command and staff had been backbriefed in detail, team members inspected, rehearsed, and test-fired weapons.

As the operators walked out to the edge of the airstrip, their Air Force MH-53J Pave Low sat next to the staging area like a giant sleeping prehistoric creature. Situated some 20 meters from the primary staging area, a second gray Pave Low was also being readied for the mission. One crucial practice in special operations planning is 100-percent redundancy. Operators do not cherish the thought of a one-way trip, and this group was no different. The second aircraft would accompany the infiltration as backup. Inside were para-rescue and combat-control special operators from the Air Force's Special Operations Command. Their mission was to aid in a follow-on infiltration if the primary aircraft went down or to assist in extraction if the landing zone (LZ) was hot and the mission had to be aborted.

As the team became accustomed to the desert night, the Pave Low's crew made its final checks. Under the glare of red lights, the command pilot and McAlister covered last-minute details, procedures, checkpoints, and code words. The copilot then reviewed emergency actions and procedures with the crew and team members.

The team lifted its A-III packs and secured its weapons. Two men carried Heckler & Koch MP5 SD3 submachine guns, a silenced version of the sturdy 9mm submachine gun that's essential for silent elimination of an enemy. The remainder of the team carried AKM47s, a reliable folding-stock version of the venerable Kalashnikov assault rifle

An airman aboard an MH-60G Pave Hawk peers through night-vision goggles during operations in Iraq.

commonly found in hands of Iraqi civilians. The only light came from the helicopter's red interior lights. Big Mac, George, Ra-Ra, Jumpmaster, Tom, and Jesus (pronounced hey-zeus) walked up the ramp in reverse order, sat down opposite each other, and buckled their seatbelts. Eight red nylon troop seats, four to a side, sat at the rear of the aircraft.

Big Mac sat down, put on the combination earphones/microphone, and made a communications check with the pilot. He scanned the dim interior, noting the positions of the right and left gunners. McAlister noted that team members were wearing their ear plugs and holding their weapons between their knees, muzzle down. The team settled into its seats and tried to relax.

Infiltration

The team's low-level flight to the LZ felt like a rollercoaster ride but was otherwise uneventful. As the helicopter streaked past the various checkpoints, the pilot notified Mac. In turn, Mac passed this critical information to the team members. Checkpoint information dated back to World War II operations when members of Britain's Special Operations Executive (SOE) and the American Office of Strategic Services (OSS) were informed of current locations in the event they had to bail out before the designated release

A B-2 stealth bomber at Whiteman Air Force Base, Missouri, moments before it lifts off for a precision strike in Iraq.

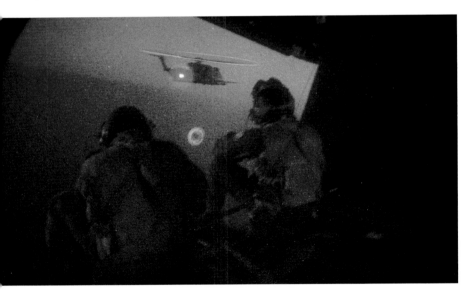

Airmen aboard an MH-53J Pave Low observe a sister ship during night refueling operations.

glided into the landing zone with its nose flaring slightly high. At this point, the follow-on helicopter took up a racetrack flight pattern in preparation to support extraction efforts if required. NVGs were not reliable in the dust storm the Pave Low was creating, so each operator wore standard-issue dust goggles. As the MH-53J bounced to a halt, the first two operators raced down the ramp into the talcum dust and peeled off in opposite directions to take up defensive positions 15 meters from the aircraft. The rest of the team followed.

Assault packs were thrown to the desert floor, and operators fell in behind with weapons pointed into the darkness. The Pave Low lurched into the night sky, made a sharp turn to port, and headed for home. Within seconds, the chopper was gone and only silence surrounded the team. The six men effortlessly rose as one, secured their packs, and headed southwest at a loping trot. Their pace was easy and steady, and their NVGs helped them avoid obstacles.

One hour later, the team reached the rendezvous point. While Mac rechecked his GPS, the team established 360-degree security. Then two vehicles slowly pulled up on the dirt road fronting the team's position. A woman exited from the passenger side of a beat-up Mercedes and approached their position. Knowing that she was under surveillance and likely in the sights of a silenced weapon, she made sure her movements were deliberate and slow. The ISA operative removed a small light with an IR filter from her robes and signaled with three dots and a dash. Leaving his weapon and equipment, Mac walked slowly toward the woman, who said in a distinct Brooklyn accent, "Welcome to Baghdad."

point. That way, operatives were not totally lost and stood a better chance of surviving and locating their contacts.

The infiltration was being monitored from an Air Force AWAC flying high overhead, while a pair of A-10 Warthogs lazily bore holes in the night sky. Their easy and graceful flight patterns hid the destructive power they were prepared to unleash.

Ten minutes before landing, the team was given the final checkpoint. Weapons were rechecked to confirm that rounds were in the chambers and magazines secured. The Pave Low

The team split into two three-man groups and climbed into the Mercedes and an old Volkswagen van for the short drive into the city. Iraqis were starting the day with the traditional Muslim calls to prayer as the vehicles entered a run-down garage at a safe house, where they were met by the rest of the ISA reception committee. The ISA team had been in the city for several weeks; they had procured safe houses, transportation, water, food, and information. The DELTA operators were shown to rooms where sleeping pallets were positioned. They tried to rest while the reception team handled the security duties. Even with security duties handled by ISA, one DELTA operative was always alert. Security responsibilities cannot be delegated.

You Can Run, But You Can't Hide

At 1930 hours, the team reviewed the operation for the last time. Moving to the vehicles, four operatives loaded into the green VW van while the other two got into the Mercedes. The vehicles cruised through the streets, avoiding military checkpoints and, after an hour, arrived at a closed tobacco shop one city block from a restaurant frequented by Hussein and his henchmen. The restaurant (and the entire city block) was built atop a deep underground bunker nearly 20 years earlier, during the Iran–Iraq war. Not known to this particular team, several other of Hussein's hangouts were also being "serviced" throughout the city. Big Mac's team was infiltrated to this recently discovered location because of specific intelligence information that a meeting was to take place.

The team took position on the roof of the three-story shop and established satellite communications with the squadron. Team members took turns watching the target area through a rubber-coated spotter scope. All they could do was wait—and not be discovered by the Iraqis.

At 2330 hours the activity on the streets below began to subside. Ra-Ra, the communications specialist, sat hunched over his compact SATCOM. The earpiece crackled as the weapons officer onboard a B-2 bomber made his initial contact with the team after a 14-hour flight from Whiteman Air Force Base in Missouri. It lazily orbited the sprawling city, silent and unseen, on the chance that one of the teams would site the Ace of Spades. Contained in its high-tech belly was a bunker buster, a second-generation smart bomb designed to penetrate deeply into the earth and destroy bunker systems.

With virtually no activity on the street below, a motor home and its SUV escorts pulled in front of the targeted restaurant. Only Hussein and the most senior Iraqi officials were known to use motor homes to move around in comfort and anonymity. The convoy was easily seen by George, who kept his eyes on the target and raised a thumbs up signal with his left hand.

Ra-Ra bent over to where Big Mac lay stretched out on the roof. "Contact," he said, and the team moved slowly into position. The B-2 was notified while Jesus painted an invisible laser marker on the restaurant. "Target is marked," said Ra-Ra, as he passed the information to the now-incoming bomber and stood by for notification of bomb release. Within seconds, the B-2

A soldier provides outer security during a raid in Kirkuk.

notified the team of the bomb's release. For approximately two minutes, the bomb glided toward the earth and its target.

With astounding shock and power, the bunker buster slammed into the ground, driving deep into the earth and exploding. Although they were a city block away, the team members bounced up and down on the roof like so many ping pong balls. After the shockwave and tremendous explosion, the team was soon threatened by falling debris.

Mac and Jesus peered through the dust with their scope and binoculars and were astonished to see a large crater at least 50 meters in circumference. Mac gave Ra-Ra the thumbs up, and the message was transmitted to the bomber: "Target destroyed. Out."

The team assessed the destruction and policed the area while waiting for the confusion in the street below to build. In groups of two, they made their way to the ground floor where they were met by an ISA operative. All six DELTA troopers piled into a Mercedes and exited the area with due haste. Pandemonium reigned in the streets, but such extreme confusion offered a better chance of avoiding security forces.

The ISA operative exited the vehicle at a pre-arranged location and Tom got behind the wheel. Approaching the desert, Tom dropped off the road onto a deserted track northwest of the city and continued as far as possible before the Mercedes became mired in deep sand. Piling out of the car, the team shouldered the packs and weapons and, after a quick check of men, equipment, and their position, the team moved out at the casual trot they knew so well. Next stop, the pickup zone (PZ), and with luck and skill, an uneventful ride to Kuwait.

Mission accomplished—or was it?

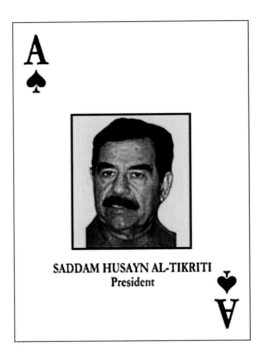

Saddam Hussein, "Ace of Spades" in central command's deck of most-wanted cards distributed throughout Iraq.

Ace of Spades

Task Force 121 was initially established in Afghanistan to hunt down bin Laden's al Qaeda and Taliban allies and to complement the Special Operations Forces participating in Operation *Iraqi Freedom*. Its assets come from the best operatives of the joint special operations community. Elements from the 10th Special Forces Group, 160th Special Operations Aviation Regiment, SEAL Team Six, and DELTA provide the on-the-ground commanders with a potent strike force for counterterrorist operations or a precision snatch team to capture or neutralize high-payoff targets (HPTs).

For many years, special operators from DELTA had been searching for and securing war crime suspects in the Balkans. The tactics, techniques, and procedures perfected in that dismal theater of operations were brought to bear in another theater where misery, death, and hatred ruled supreme.

At Baghdad International Airport, Warrant Officer 3 Pat Hamilton, a veteran of 20 years, had just eased his massive frame into a folding chair in front of the team's portable computer when he heard the squadron's executive officer (XO), who was acting as liaison to Task Force 121, let out a squeal of delight. Holding the satellite phone away from his mouth, he yelled, "Hot damn! Hey Chief, round up the team. Intel indicates that the Ace of Spades has been located! *Red Dawn* is a go!"

With that information, the hanger became a hub of intense activity as the Task Force 121 operators policed up their equipment, which had been placed in individual piles for easy access.

Operation *Red Dawn* is one of the finest examples of special operations, conventional forces, and external agencies working in close cooperation and coordination to successfully accomplish a very sensitive mission. The term "Ace of Spades" refers to the position Saddam Hussein occupies in a specially produced deck of cards containing pictures of the 52 most wanted Iraqis.

Colonel Jim Hickey, Commander of the 4th Division's Raider Brigade, was the man with the target pinned on his back. The weight on the officer's shoulders was massive—it was his job to capture Hussein alive. The command structure, from the White House down to the commanding general, did not wish to explain to the world why another operation had resulted in the death of a Hussein family member. The highly publicized deaths of Saddam Hussein's two sons had taken place just months earlier when U.S. forces attempted to take them captive.

Rat in a Hole

Launching in blackout configuration and using NVGs, special operations aviation assets skimmed over the dark Iraqi terrain. Like angry bumblebees, the MH-6 Little Birds descended into landing zones around a farm near Ad Dawr, due south of Saddam Hussein's tribal sanctuary of Tikrit. The farm had been searched before, but only after a great deal of information analysis and the interrogation of numerous subjects had Hussein's possible hiding place been revealed by an informant and targeted.

Springing from their seats on the sides of the MH-6s, Task Force 121 soldiers quickly moved into supporting positions, where they could cover the areas being searched by members of the raider brigade. Each operator carried a modified Colt M4 chambered in 5.56mm that was factory modified with low-visibility rear sights, laser sights, and high-intensity flashlights controlled from the shooter's pistol grip.

The immediate area reminded Chief Hamilton of a laser light show at a rock concert. But only one color—red—was visible. This vision was soon shattered by the crackle of radio transmissions. Saddam Hussein's hole had been found!

Soldiers stood with weapons ready as the styrofoam plug was removed, revealing an unkempt individual. Rising slowly out of the hole, hands held high, the man reportedly said in Arabic: "I am Saddam Hussein. I am president of Iraq, and I am willing to negotiate." Even in defeat, this tyrant, whose heroes were Hitler and Stalin, still felt he was in control. However, a special operator dispelled any thoughts concerning who was in charge. "President Bush sends his regards," he calmly replied. Saddam Hussein was pulled from his hole and searched. His 9mm pistol was removed from his belt and a grateful President Bush stated in a television speech that it was presented to him by DELTA troopers. As Hussein was being prepared for transportation, he became belligerent and spit in a soldier's face. His attempt to resist brought Chief Hamilton out of the shadows, and Hussein went down with several other operators assisting. He was restrained with flex cuffs and an empty sandbag placed over his head. Moving with the swift action gained only through countless hours of rehearsals, the operators strapped the Ace of Spades into an MH-6 for a hasty exfiltration.

A prisoner processing point was established at Saddam Hussein's palace in Tikrit, and the MH-6 landed in a heavily guarded area. Before the bird had fully landed, Hussein was offloaded and rushed into a medical receiving area, where special forces medical personnel, along with combat photographers, thoroughly searched and photographed the dictator.

The initial concern for those guarding Hussein was that he would attempt suicide. So Hussein received the royal treatment—a full body cavity search for suicide pills. After all, his idol, Hitler, was among the notable Nazis who cheated the hangman's noose. After the inspection, he was given a quick physical, fingerprinted, photographed, and bundled back onto a chopper for a fast ride to Baghdad.

The airspace was alive with all manner of gunships, SIGINT-collecting helicopters, and UH-60s carrying reaction forces. In a secluded, heavily guarded aircraft parking area, an MC-130 Combat Talon stood ready to depart. Eight seasoned veterans casually stood 60 feet away from the Talon making small talk. The easygoing atmosphere was shattered when a member of the Special Operations Combat Control Team ran to the area where the chopper was to land. Yelling over his left shoulder, "six minutes out!" was all the team needed to move into position near the LZ. Armed with pistols, the team prepared to escort Saddam Hussein to his flight.

The chopper landed perfectly. As soon as the door opened, Hussein was transferred to four sets of waiting hands. His feet barley touched the ground as he was whisked up the rear ramp into the waiting aircraft's cavernous cargo bay. The team secured him in a seat as the ramp came up, and the aircraft began its taxi

Saddam Hussein is subdued after becoming "uncooperative" during his capture. The President-for-life and Chairman of the Revolutionary Command Council, Hussein began to argue and was brought down after he spit in a trooper's face.

After his apprehension, Saddam Hussein was brought into a temporary holding area in Tikrit.

for takeoff. Without stopping, the Combat Talon roared onto the runway and into the clear darkness of the Arabian night.

As the Talon flew out of sight, Chief Hamilton leaned back against his aircraft, spit some snuff out the side of his mouth, and said to no one in particular, "Wish we'd nailed that S.O.B last time." In some ways, the victory seemed hollow, but in retrospect, they all felt the same sense of loss, the same sense of pride, and the same sense of accomplishment.

"Hell," Hamilton said as he and his team slowly headed toward the hanger that was their home, "What I need is a cold beer."

Mission accomplished.

Epilogue

After many years of studying the art of insurgency and its subset, terrorism, it's fair to say that in the future, the world may have an opportunity to observe counterterrorist operations executed by DELTA, but most of their missions will be executed with surgical precision, and the public will never hear of their accomplishments.

In a box of mementos from campaigns, battles, and counterterrorist operations, a battered and scratched lighter bears the following engraved sentiment: "Live by chance, Love by choice, Kill by profession."

Willing to do whatever it takes to achieve their goals, 1st Special Forces Operational Detachment–DELTA is ready.

Index